The Decline in Saving

The Decline in Saving

A Threat to America's Prosperity?

Barry P. Bosworth

BROOKINGS INSTITUTION PRESS
Washington, D.C.

Library of Congress Cataloging-in-Publication data
Bosworth, Barry, 1942–
   The Decline in Saving : A Threat to America's Prosperity? / Barry P. Bosworth.
     p. cm.
   Includes bibliographical references and index.
   Summary: "Examines the decline in saving in the United States over the
past quarter-century. Is it a statistical artifact of the official measure of saving?
Why don't Americans save? What are the consequences for economic growth,
the performance of the aggregate economy, and policy goals?"—Provided by
publisher.
   ISBN 978-0-8157-2135-2 (pbk. : alk. paper)
   1. Saving and investment—United States. 2. United States—Economic policy.
I. Title.
   HC110.S3B668 2011
   339.4'30973—dc23   2011049589

9 8 7 6 5 4 3 2 1

Printed on acid-free paper

Typeset in Sabon

Composition by Cynthia Stock
Silver Spring, Maryland

Printed by R. R. Donnelley
Harrisonburg, Virginia

Contents

Foreword

The large decline in the U.S. household saving rate over the past quarter-century has puzzled many economists. Americans have long been known for having a relatively low rate of saving, but the depth to which saving fell in the middle of the first decade of the twenty-first century was unprecedented among modern industrial economies. Why don't Americans save? While a variety of hypotheses have been advanced, considerable disagreement persists. At the same time, many observers were surprised that the consequences of low household saving seemed so benign. The rate of capital investment and economic growth actually accelerated in the 1990s as foreign capital inflows offset reduced domestic saving and technological innovations stretched the value of investment spending. Many studies have also concluded that despite reduced rates of saving, there is little evidence of a growing problem of inadequate preparation for retirement and that poverty rates of older Americans have continued to decline.

In this study, Barry Bosworth examines the causes and consequences of low saving from several perspectives. First, to what extent is the fall in saving simply a statistical artifact of the official measure of saving, which ignores important dimensions of saving and investment in a modern economy? Second, why has saving behavior changed in the United States? The failure of saving rates to rise as the baby boom generation moved into its peak earning years has shifted the focus away from demographic explanations to a greater emphasis on the role of wealth. Third, what can be learned from observing saving behavior in other advanced economies and in high-growth emerging markets? And, finally, what have been the consequences of low saving for economic growth, the performance of the aggregate economy, and other policy goals?

These issues are likely to take on even greater importance in the aftermath of the financial crisis as Americans feel pressure to cut back and live within their means. The collapse of asset prices has made households feel less wealthy than they did just a few years ago. There has been a modest increase in the rate of household saving, but it has been more than offset by an extraordinary rise in government borrowing, and the nation now has a negative national saving rate. The country struggles to shift away from a decades-long emphasis on consumption toward a renewed commitment to production and export to the rest of the world. The aging of the baby boom generation and the costs of boomers' retirement make that change even more difficult.

The preparation of this book was financed by a grant from the Smith-Richardson Foundation. Previous research for the project benefited from financial support provided by the Social Security Administration to the Center on Retirement Research at Boston College and from grants from the Nomura Foundation. The author is grateful to several anonymous referees for very helpful comments and suggestions and to Sveta Milusheva, Maria Ramrath, and Rosanna Smart, who provided extensive research assistance.

KAREN DYNAN
Vice President and Co-Director
of Economic Studies

Brookings Institution
December 2011

CHAPTER ONE

Introduction

Over the past quarter-century, rates of saving in the United States have fallen precipitously, and in the aftermath of the 2008–09 financial crisis, the nation's saving rate has turned negative. Even before the onset of the crisis, net national saving amounted to only 2 percent of the nation's income, while the average was 11 percent in the three decades before 1980. In effect, Americans have been engaged in a long-running spending spree, consuming their incomes at an unsustainable rate in both the public and private sectors. The shift toward a consumption-based economy is evident in the rising share of gross domestic product (GDP) allocated to consumption. The consumption share, which had long been virtually constant at 62–63 percent of GDP, began to rise in the early 1980s, and it is currently in excess of 70 percent (figure 1-1). This profligacy has been evident at both the government and the individual household level. In the public sector, the lack of saving and investment has been reflected in an erosion of the nation's public infrastructure and, but for a brief period in the late 1990s, increasing levels of public indebtedness. At the household level, the average saving rate declined to 1 percent of income before surging to about 5 percent amid the panic of the financial crisis. Even this heightened rate of household saving, hailed as a major turnaround, is less than half the rate achieved in the decades prior to 1980. At the beginning of the 1980s, the United States was the world's largest creditor nation, with a net international investment position of $360 billion, equal to 15 percent of national income. By 2010, it was the world's largest debtor. The nation's international liabilities have come to exceed its assets by more than $3 trillion—about 5 percent of the nation's net wealth, or 25 percent of national income.

Figure 1-1. *Personal Consumption as a Percent of GDP, 1951–2010*

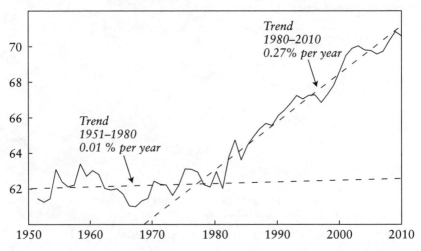

Sources: Bureau of Economic Analysis (2011a, table 1.1.5) and author's calculations.

This shift in behavior has received mixed reviews, both international and domestic. On the one hand, U. S. consumer markets have been the engine for global economic growth because other countries could rely on exports to the United States to drive the expansion of their economies. The strength of the U.S. market, for example, supported reliance on export-promotion policies as a primary means of recovery from the 1997–98 Asian financial crisis. The expansion of exports to the United States also provided an important impetus for the economic awakening of vast portions of the world's poorest countries, marked particularly by the gains in China and India. Yet outside observers have long been uneasy about the magnitude of the payments imbalance between the United States and the rest of the world, and they were often critical of Americans' low saving rate during a period in which they nevertheless took full advantage of strong U.S. markets for consumer goods.

Within the United States, the strength of domestic consumer markets was a major contributor to a long episode of sustained economic growth and job creation; the unemployment rate fell to levels that were previously thought to be unsustainable. From many perspectives, the performance of the U.S. economy in the 1990s did seem like the best of times. However, the boom also concealed some of the underlying problems.

Governments, in particular, became highly dependent on transitory tax revenues from the capital gains associated with the surge in equity and real estate markets. The collapse of revenues in the recent financial crisis has left all levels of government with large shortfalls reflected in huge budget deficits (negative saving) in the short run and curtailment of public investment over a longer period. Households also came to rely on debt financing for significant portions of their consumption, supported in turn by rising home prices. That support vanished in the wealth losses of 2008–09. Going forward, many Americans will have to focus on rebuilding their financial balance sheets, something that will require more saving and less consumption for a sustained period.

This book provides a review of both the causes and consequences of the decline in American saving. To begin, the magnitude of the two-decade-long fall in household saving has been truly astonishing; it is even more surprising in view of the fact that the large cohort of baby boomers should have been in their peak saving years. The reasons for that reduced saving have generated considerable controversy within the research literature, as have the measures used to calculate saving. But equally significant is the fact that many of the predicted consequences of low saving have not been evident. For example, a fall in saving would be expected to curb the nation's rate of capital accumulation and slow the pace of economic growth, but that has not been the case: domestic investment was strong and the rate of productivity growth accelerated in the years between the mid-1990s and the onset of the financial crisis. A low rate of saving should imply reduced rates of household wealth accumulation. Yet the net worth of American households grew at unprecedented rates, and as recently as 2008 several analyses suggested that those approaching retirement were in significantly better financial condition than prior generations.

Why has saving declined, and why have the consequences been so benign? Those are the key questions that this book seeks to address. The issues have been made even more complex by the severity of the 2008–09 financial crisis. The crisis itself cannot be traced to low saving, but adjusting to a more balanced path to economic growth with a higher, more sustainable rate of saving than in the past will be more difficult and painful because of the depth of the global economic decline. The original objective was to shift a portion of U.S. production out of the domestic market for consumption goods and into the export markets in an equally fast-growing global economy. Over several years and with a coordinated change in the policies of other countries, the rebalancing of the U.S.

economy could have been accomplished without significant disruption. Today, households are saving more, but it is against the backdrop of a domestic economy propped up by large government deficits and a global economy in which many nations see increased exports as the offset to weak domestic demand. The achievement of a future of strong and balanced economic growth has become much more difficult.

Alternative Saving Measures

The discussion begins in chapter 2 with a review of the official national income and product accounts measures of saving in the United States, which are those that show the precipitous fall of saving in both the private and the public sectors. Yet those measures are not universally accepted, and some critics challenge the concept of saving that is used in the national accounts. They argue that the definitions of saving and investment are too narrow, in that they ignore investments in consumer durables, health, education, research and development, and other intangibles. Furthermore, the treatment of capital gains/losses—their exclusion from saving but inclusion as a component of wealth change—is a source of considerable confusion and controversy. To a large extent the confusion reflects the failure to distinguish between the macroeconomic perspective, with its emphasis on measuring the nation's total production and its distribution, and the microeconomic perspective, with its focus on measuring the economic well-being of individual households. Although the rise in household wealth associated with the boom in equity and home prices appeared as saving at the individual level, it did not represent an increase in resources that could be used to finance capital investments.

Similarly, we could broaden the range of expenditures that we classify as investment and thereby raise the reported saving rate. Many of those suggestions have merit but stumble on difficulties in measurement. For example, the pursuit of a college degree should be seen as an investment activity, but studies of how students spend their time suggest that there is also a significant consumption component, and we are uncertain about how to separate the two. One objective of chapter 2 is to provide a conceptual framework for thinking about the adequacy of saving and investment and to evaluate the implications of the differing proposed measures of saving. An important conclusion is that the broader definitions of saving and investment proposed would not fundamentally change the narrative of a secularly diminished rate of saving in the United States.

The national accounts data can be used to separate national saving into its public and private components and, in the private sector, to distinguish between the saving of households and businesses. As we shall see, the various components of saving show quite different secular and cyclical patterns. However, some analysts argue that the divisions are meaningless since households are the owners of businesses, which save and invest as the households' agents, and taxpayer households ultimately bear the burden of paying for the government's activities. They argue, for example, that efforts to increase national saving by reducing the dissaving of government will simply be offset by compensating actions by households. The issue of which measures of saving are most appropriate is of great importance in explaining why saving has declined and of even more importance in determining what, if anything, can be done about it. This issue is an important aspect of the next chapter, and it arises again in the discussion in later chapters of the reasons for the decline in saving and its consequences.

Why Has Household Saving Fallen?

Chapter 3 focuses more directly on the question of why the rate of household saving has fallen. The decline, which first emerged in the 1980s, accelerated during the 1990s, and saving remained very low right up to the onset of the financial crisis. The chapter both examines the evidence on potential reasons for the falloff from the macroeconomic perspective and analyzes microsurvey data from individual households. At the aggregate level, the analyses have tended to highly confirm a strong influence from unusually large capital gains on wealth and easier access to credit. The capital gains were concentrated in corporate equities and the housing market. Innovations in the mortgage market greatly increased the ease with which homeowners could extract equity from the appreciating value of their homes.

The sharp rise in the household saving rate in the aftermath of the financial crisis supports the role of wealth effects and credit availability, but too little time has passed to fully distinguish those effects from the short-term trauma of the crisis itself. The change to a higher rate of household saving has also been somewhat inopportune since it has occurred along with a collapse in domestic investment and difficulty in expanding exports. After several decades, it has not been easy to shift away from a consumption-oriented economy. Therefore, the rise in household saving has been more than offset by an extraordinary increase in public dissaving as the government struggles to rebalance the economy.

The study is less successful in using the microsurvey data to identify the socioeconomic characteristics of households that changed their saving behavior. While it is possible to show the broad nature of the wealth gains across households of varying characteristics, efforts to separate those gains into their saving and valuation components—active versus passive saving—are afflicted with large measurement errors. Similarly, households cannot recall their consumption outlays with sufficient accuracy to measure saving as income minus consumption.

International Saving Patterns

Variations in the international experience are taken up in chapter 4. Reductions in the barriers to trade across borders and the expansion of international capital transactions have promoted a much more open global economy in which the patterns of saving and investment in other countries have major implications for the United States. The examination of cross-national experiences also yields richer data with which to explore the determinants of saving behavior. Consideration of the global pattern of saving and investment highlights the magnitude of the U.S. imbalance. The global perspective has been the basis of the claim by some U.S. economists that the problem is not that the United States saves too little, but that others save too much. Both phenomena played important roles in contributing to the pattern of a consumption-based boom in the United States, large external imbalances between the United States and Asia, asset market bubbles, and the excesses that led to the 2008–09 financial crisis. At the same time, consideration of saving and investment trends in individual countries or groups of countries highlights the diversity of experiences. Among the high-income countries, special attention is devoted to Canada, Japan, and Europe for the insights that they might offer to the United States. China and India illustrate the much different experience within emerging markets and their increasing influence on trends in the global economy.

Canada is of interest because it shares many of the institutional and cultural features of the United States, yet at least in the 1970s and 1980s, saving rates there evolved quite differently. More recently, however, the Canadian household saving rate fell as sharply as that of the United States, but saving within the corporate sector rose by an amount more than sufficient to offset the reduced rate of household saving, leaving private saving unchanged. Canada also stands out for the progress that it has made in bringing its public sector budget into balance. Both Canada and the United States have experienced little or no change in demographic structure over the past two decades, and while Canadian home prices rose less than those in the United States, the two countries shared large valuation gains on corporate equities and a common downward trend in real rates of interest. Also, the mortgage market innovations that led to the growth of the subprime mortgage market in the United States were largely absent from Canada.

The magnitude of the fall in saving within Japan is even larger than that in the United States, but the explanations of the declines have little in common. Japanese researchers attribute the reduced saving to population aging, which is largely absent in the United States and Canada; moreover, Japan has experienced major losses, not gains, in asset markets. Like Canada, Japan has had a major increase in corporate saving, but its public sector dissaving resembles that of the United States. The Japanese investment rate also plummeted after its financial crisis and never recovered. Europe illustrates yet another distinct experience. Saving rates there have fallen less than in other high-income economies. The extent of population aging in Europe lies between that of North America and Japan, and the magnitude of the increase in the wealth-income ratio is quite variable and its correlation with saving less than in the United States.

The acceleration of economic growth in China and India has been accompanied by remarkable increases in domestic rates of saving. It seems evident that the rapid rates of income growth there have exerted a strong positive impact on saving. Until recently, the increased saving was matched by an equally rapid expansion of domestic capital formation. Since the Asian financial crisis of 1997–98, however, several countries within East Asia, including China, have experienced a significant moderation of investment and the emergence of large current account surpluses that are the principal offsets to the U.S deficits. The diversity of international experience would seem to offer a rich set of data to distinguish among the competing hypotheses for saving behavior, but the comparisons are complicated by the varying quality of data and major differences in the underlying institutions that determine saving. It seems unlikely that a single model or a simple set of explanations can account for the wide variations in country experiences, but the international review does not yield any glaring contradiction of an explanation of the reduced U.S. rate of saving that emphasizes wealth changes and the liberalization of credit. The added feature is the importance of income growth–particularly in developing economies—as a positive influence on saving.

The Consequences of Low Saving

To date, the low rate of saving has had surprisingly benign effects on Americans, but that may be in the process of changing. Historically, economists and other public commentators have expressed concern about the implications of low rates of saving in three different dimensions, which are addressed in more detail in chapter 5. First, within the macroeconomic context, saving has been emphasized as a necessary means of financing capital accumulation and economic growth. This view was reinforced by studies such as Feldstein and Horioka (1980), which pointed to the high correlation between domestic saving and investment as evidence of the limited development of international capital markets and a restricted ability to finance large external imbalances. This closed-economy interpretation led to concerns that reduced domestic saving or large budget deficits would crowd out investment and negatively impact the nation's economic growth. In today's world, however, the Feldstein-Horioka finding is of reduced relevance; investment can be financed with equal ease with either domestic or foreign saving, and there is little evidence that low rates of domestic saving have crowded out investment.

Instead, a low rate of saving relative to investment is reflected in a large external deficit with the rest of the world. The sustainability of the external deficit is the second dimension of concern to consider when examining the implications of low rates of saving. In effect, the United States borrows from abroad or sells assets to finance its current spending. In the process, it has accumulated a high level of net external indebtedness, about 25 percent of GDP. This level of debt is already beyond the magnitude at which other countries encountered financing problems. Perhaps the U.S. position as a reserve currency and its tradition of strong enforcement of commercial contracts gives it some additional leeway. Thus far, in terms of interest rate premiums on U.S. government debt, there is no evidence of a significant foreign concern with a U.S. default.

Estimates of the large adjustments required in exchange rates and an extraordinary public sector deficit both suggest, however, that restoration of a more balanced financial position would bring about major reductions in the terms of trade and American standards of living. The magnitude of the recession and the drop in domestic demand has resulted in a substantial reduction in the external deficit, but the United States continues to have difficulty reinventing a significant export capability.

Finally, low rates of household saving over an extended period should raise fears about the adequacy of households' preparation for retirement. However, again there is surprisingly little evidence of a growing problem. The economic position of the elderly has improved substantially during the period of falling national saving. A surprisingly large number of Americans make no significant financial preparation for retirement, relying instead on ownership of a home and Social Security benefits in their retirement years. Among higher-income groups the lower rate of saving did not translate into reduced wealth for retirement because of the remarkable price appreciation in asset markets. Capital gains were more than sufficient to offset the reduced saving. Many research studies prior to the financial crisis suggested a rather benign financial outlook for older Americans.

Again, however, the situation may be changing in the aftermath of the financial crisis. It brought the asset market boom of the last twenty years to an end, and asset prices are regressing toward a more normal historical level. Ultimately, the new equilibrium level of asset prices will depend on the extent and timing of recovery in the macroeconomic economy. In addition, the magnitude of the fiscal deficit is likely to require the scaling back of transfers to the elderly in the future, making them more dependent on their own financial resources. Surveys from the post-crisis period that cover the financial situation of retired and near-retired individuals have yet to become available; however, a combination of large wealth losses and a very low interest rate on annuities should translate into significantly lower retirement incomes than anticipated before the crisis. One response may be for older workers to continue working and delay retirement.

CHAPTER TWO

Measuring Saving

Much of the controversy and confusion about the adequacy of current rates of saving centers around different notions of what constitutes saving. Most simply, "saving" is defined as the portion of income that is not spent on consumption, but that definition still leaves room for considerable argument over precisely what should be included.

The standard measures of national saving and its components—government and private saving and, within the private sector, household and corporate saving—are all derived from the national accounts. The national income and product accounts (NIPAs) are designed to provide a coherent framework for measuring the nation's total production and the distribution of the income derived from that production.[1] To a close approximation, those accounts are now also consistent with the national accounting systems of other countries, enabling international comparisons of saving behavior. Within the NIPAs, national saving measures the portion of total production (income) that is set aside—not consumed—and used to finance investment. It is a key indicator of the extent to which the nation is using resources today for purposes of increasing future production and incomes.

A country's GDP, defined as the market value of all goods and services produced for final demand within the country for a given time period,

---

1. The national accounts include all production of goods, whether supplied to others or for own consumption, while services are included only if they are supplied to others. Thus, the production of agricultural products by farm families for their own consumption is included, but the household production of services is included only if services are performed by a paid staff. The asymmetric treatment of services is mainly a historical development that can be traced to the lack of data about the activities of household members.

equals the sum of public and private consumption expenditures (C), investment (I), and exports (X), minus imports (M):

$$(1) \qquad\qquad GDP = C + I + X - M.$$

National saving can then be defined as GDP minus consumption or, equivalently, saving equals investment plus net exports to the rest of the world:

$$(2) \qquad\qquad S = I + (X - M).$$

The situation is slightly more complex in practice because the residents of a country can earn income from overseas activity as well as domestic production. Thus, the national accounts distinguish between gross domestic product (GDP) and gross national income (GNI), where GNI includes net earnings from abroad. The result is a small redefinition of national saving,

$$(3) \qquad\qquad (GNI - C) = S = I + CA,$$

in which the difference between domestic saving and investment is equal to the current account balance (CA) of the United States with the rest of the world. It is also common to measure income, saving, and investment net of allowances for the depreciation of existing capital.[2] Within this construct, it is relatively simple to disaggregate further to distinguish between public (government) and private sector saving and, within the latter, between household and corporate saving. Equation (3) provides the framework for the summary of saving trends shown in table 2-1.

It is this formulation of national saving and its composition that is the basis for concerns about low and declining rates of saving. At the national level, the difference between national saving and domestic investment, the current account, is often used as a summary measure of the nation's dependence on foreign sources of financing, and large cumulative current

2. It is common in the advanced economies to focus on measures of income and saving after deduction of depreciation allowances, but the accurate assessment of depreciation on existing capital is a complex issue and many developing countries are content to produce estimates of gross incomes and saving. Hence, many of the international comparisons rely on gross saving.

Table 2-1. *Net Saving and Investment Balance by Sector*
Percent of national income

Item	1970–79	1980–89	1990–99	2000–07	2008–10
Gross domestic investment	22.9	23.4	21.2	22.2	18.4
Capital consumption allowances	12.4	14.1	13.3	13.7	14.9
Net investment	10.6	9.4	7.9	8.4	3.5
Net national saving	9.6	6.5	5.4	3.7	–0.7
Government saving	–1.4	–3.6	–2.4	–1.7	–8.7
Federal	–2.2	–3.9	–2.6	–1.7	–8.3
State and local	0.8	0.4	0.2	0.0	–0.5
Private saving	11.0	10.0	7.8	5.4	8.0
Personal (household) saving	7.7	7.2	4.7	2.4	4.6
Corporate retained earnings	3.4	2.9	3.2	3.0	3.4
Net foreign lending (current account)	0.2	–1.8	–1.7	–5.4	–4.1
Statistical discrepancy	1.1	1.1	0.8	–0.7	0.2

Source: Bureau of Economic Analysis (2011a, tables 1.7.5 and 5.1).

account deficits reflect the growing net indebtedness of the United States to the rest of the world. At the household level, the failure to save can endanger a family's economic security, both in compensating for spells of income loss (precautionary saving) and old age (retirement saving).

Both of these concerns are evident in table 2-1. The household saving rate has decreased from a relatively steady 10 percent of national income in the decades prior to 1980 to an average of 2 percent in the seven years prior to the financial crisis. Corporate saving, which many would add to that of households on the basis that households are the ultimate owners of businesses, shows no secular trend, but the national saving rate has fallen even more than the household rate because of the increased frequency and severity of public sector budget deficits. Thus, the national saving rate fell from 12 percent in the 1970s to an average of only 3.5 percent in the years before the financial crisis. That amount was insufficient to finance the nation's investment opportunities, and the United States has become increasingly reliant on foreign sources of saving. The current account deficit has averaged in excess of 5 percent of national income over the past decade, and it is this deficit that has led to comments about "American profligacy."

Yet not everyone accepts these measures of the nation's saving and investment. The system of national accounts, for example, reflects a number of conceptual and definitional decisions that have created controversy. First, because of the focus on measuring current production and the flow of incomes from that production, the income measures of the national accounts exclude the gains and losses that accrue to owners of existing assets as the result of changes in asset prices. In recent decades, however, variations in asset values have been far more important than saving as a source of change in household wealth, and some economists would like to incorporate those variations directly into the definition of saving. Furthermore, the rate of inflation has changed substantially over the past three decades, and that can also have major distorting effects on reported measures of net asset income and saving.

Second, there is an extensive literature arguing that the standard definition of investment used in the national accounts capital is too narrow and that a broader definition would significantly affect the measures of U.S. saving/investment performance both over time and in the comparison with those of other countries. Part of the debate revolves around the boundary between consumption and investment in the classification of products. The most obvious example is that of expenditures on consumer durables, which produce a stream of services extending into the future rather than being fully consumed in the current period. Some economists would like to group expenditures on consumer durables with those on housing as a form of investment. A closely related set of concerns arises from the treatment of expenditures on intangibles (such as research and development, employee training, organizational change, and marketing expenses) as intermediate expenses in the production of other goods, rather than as capital investments.[3] The proposed accounting changes, if they increase or reduce investment, will have corresponding effects on saving. In the following sections, these definitional issues are discussed in greater detail.

3. Historically, we would have included computer software as one of those intermediate products that might be recognized as an investment. However, the U.S. national accounts were revised in 1999 to incorporate expenditures on computer software as capital investment. Similar changes were introduced in other countries as part of the shift to the 1993 version of the international system of national accounts.

Asset Valuation Changes

Much has been written about the low and falling rate of national saving seen in the national accounts, yet other statistics show a sharp rise in the nation's wealth-income ratio. If Americans save so little, why are they so rich? The divergence arises because the conventional measure of saving excludes all forms of capital gains; however, for many years prior to the financial crisis, Americans experienced large and sustained capital gains on real estate and their holdings of corporate equities. Some economists have argued that net wealth accumulation—inclusive of capital gains and losses—is a better measure of change in economic well-being than rates of saving alone, and some have argued for a redefinition of saving within the national accounts framework to include capital gains and losses.[4] Indeed, at the individual level there is much to be said for focusing on net wealth accumulation rather than saving. By enabling greater future consumption, wealth is an important element of economic well-being, and it matters little whether the individual accumulated it through saving or valuation changes.

At the aggregate level, however, the issues are more complex. The macroeconomic accounts have been expanded to include measures of accumulated wealth, and they separately identify the roles of both saving and valuation changes. Thus, the change in wealth is equal to saving plus the revaluation of existing wealth,

$$(4) \qquad W_t = W_{t-1} + (\Delta P_t/P_{t-1}) \times W_{t-1} + S,$$

where W_t is equal to wealth at time t, and $\Delta P_t/P_{t-1}$ is the change in asset prices between period t and $t - 1$. Furthermore, the national accounts framework has been extended to include a sequence of integrated accounts that trace the flow of resources from production to income and spending, to the allocation of saving between investment in physical assets and purchase of financial assets, and ultimately, combined with asset revaluations, to the change in net worth.[5] For the United States, these linkages

---

4. The issue of including capital gains/losses in the measurement of saving has been raised episodically for many decades. Some of the most cited recent references are those of Auerbach (1985), Bradford (1991), Eisner (1991), Gale and Sabelhaus (1999), Hendershott and Peek (1989), and Peach and Steindel (2000).

5. The accounting linkage between saving and wealth changes also includes some additional items, such as transfer payments to or from households and net sales of existing capital, but they are small and I ignore them in this discussion.

are documented within the flow of funds and balance sheet accounts compiled and published by the Federal Reserve. Thus, both saving and asset revaluations are shown as determinants of wealth changes without necessarily assuming that they are equivalent.

There are several reasons for distinguishing between saving and valuation changes within the national accounts. First, the primary focus of the accounts is on measuring current production and its allocation between consumption and the investment in resources that contributes to future output. By including valuation changes as part of the contribution of physical capital, we would comingle the roles of physical capital investment, other inputs, technological change, and valuation changes as contributors to the production process. While the rise in wealth that comes from rising corporate stock and real estate prices may feel like saving to individual households, it does not free up resources to invest in new capital.

Furthermore, even if we wished to focus on the change in wealth as a measure of improvement in economic well-being, its interpretation at the level of the total economy can be ambiguous. For example, increases in home values are seen as a gain to individual homeowners, but in the aggregate they largely reflect an intergenerational transfer as younger families pay higher prices to older homeowners to purchase the same flow of housing services. Some economists have gone further to argue that changes in home prices do not affect the individual household's wealth because homeownership is largely a hedge against future rent increases.[6] That is, changes in home prices reflect expectations of future rent changes, and homeownership is equivalent to the ownership of an annuity that adjusts to expectations of future rent payments. Others argue that all valuation changes, as opposed to investments in new capital, are largely transfers between individuals rather than reflections of an aggregate gain.[7]

Finally, if we included valuation changes in the definition of saving, we would have to do the same for the definition of income in order to maintain the identity that saving is equal to income minus consumption (Gale and Sabelhaus 1999). While a change in wealth may be a very important determinant of household consumption behavior, its effect is much different from that of the conventional income measure: income has

6. Examples are provided by Ortalo-Magne and Rady (2002), Sinai and Souleles (2005), and Buiter (2008).

7. See the discussion of Kuznets and others in Bhatia (1970).

large immediate effects on consumption, whereas the marginal effect of a wealth change is significantly smaller and often delayed.

On balance, there appear to be few advantages to introducing valuation changes directly into the definition of saving. Instead, the focus of national accountants has been to embed saving within a more complete framework of wealth accumulation that separately identifies the roles of both saving and valuation changes.[8] The contributions of the two factors are shown in figure 2-1 for the period of 1970 through 2009. The figure displays two measures of household wealth scaled by household income. The first is based on the reported value of net household wealth at the end of each year, inclusive of valuation effects. The second measures wealth as the cumulative sum of past saving, thereby excluding valuation changes. Valuation effects were a minor influence on total wealth until the late 1980s and 1990s. Home prices generally rose at a regular pace that was closely linked to household income; when home values increased more rapidly in the 1970s, the gains were offset by an especially weak market for corporate equities. Similarly, when the stock market surged in the early 1980s, home prices were in decline under the pressure of high mortgage interest rates. While asset price increases played a more significant role after 1985, they did not become a substantial portion of household wealth until 1995 and later.

The cumulative sum of saving was a stable multiple of disposable income (4.5) up to about 1993, but in subsequent years, the saving rate was insufficient to sustain the growth in wealth and the cumulative sum fell to 3.5 times income by 2006—a substantial decline in the contribution of saving to wealth.[9] The most striking feature, however, is that the decline in the part of wealth attributed to the cumulative sum of past saving has been more than offset by an unprecedented and sustained surge in the contribution of valuation changes (capital gains). In fact, the wealth-income ratio reached 6.6 times income at the peak of the dotcom bubble in 1999 and reached a second peak of 6.5 in 2006, just before the

8. The contrary perspective is adopted by analysts who perceive changes in equity prices as reflecting highly rational judgments about expected future productivity gains. See, for example, Hall (2000).

9. There is a statistical discrepancy between the estimate of household saving in the national accounts and that of the flow of funds because the flow of funds includes purchases of consumer durables as part of saving. The figure is based on the flow-of-funds concept to avoid any confusion between the role of the statistical discrepancy and the contribution of valuation changes.

Figure 2-1. *Household Wealth as a Ratio to Disposable Income, 1970–2010*[a]

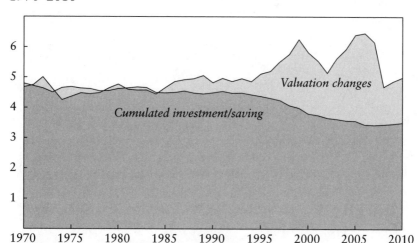

Source: Board of Governors of the Federal Reserve (2011a, tables B100 and R1900).
a. Net investment flows are converted to real values, cumulated, and then converted back to nominal values. Wealth includes consumer durables.

financial crisis. In 2006, cumulative capital gains represented nearly half of reported household wealth. Subsequently, there was a huge loss of wealth in the financial crisis, but even so the wealth-income ratio remains above its average for the 1970s and 1980s, and the real capital gains component still represented a fourth of total wealth at the end of 2010.

Capital Gains Taxation

Although the national accounts exclude income from capital gains and losses, they include any tax on realized capital gains as a deduction from current receipts in the definition of disposable income. Given that the capital gains themselves are excluded, many economists and statisticians believe that it makes more sense to treat capital gains taxes as a capital account transfer and exclude them from the definition of disposable income or saving. Estate and gift taxes, for example, have many of the same characteristics as capital gains taxes, yet they are recorded as a capital transfer. It is not clear why the tax on capital gains should be reported as a current payment when the realized capital gains/losses on which

Figure 2-2. *Personal Saving and Capital Gains Taxes, 1980–2010*

Percent of disposable income

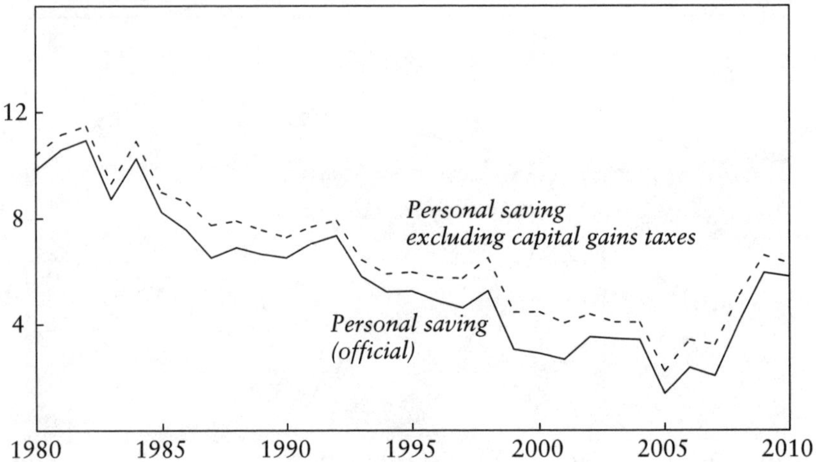

Sources: Bureau of Economic Analysis (2011a, table 2.1); Congressional Budget Office (2011, table 4-3); and author's calculations.

they are based are excluded, nor is there any obvious strong distinction between capital gains taxes and estate and gift taxes.

Estimates of realized capital gains and capital gains taxes can be obtained from income tax returns, and they are published periodically by the Treasury Department and the Congressional Budget Office. The magnitude of realized capital gains has been highly variable, and the tax rate has varied over time, but capital gains taxes were especially high— exceeding 1 percent of income—during the late 1990s when equity markets were booming (Gale and Sabelhaus 1999; Perozek and Reinsdorf 2002). Their effect on the personal saving rate is shown in figure 2-2 for the 1980–2010 period. The exclusion of capital gains taxes from the estimate of disposable income would raise the household saving rate by an average of 1 percentage point, but it would have no discernable impact on its secular decline.

Inflation

Much of the discussion of wealth effects on consumption and saving abstracts from the change in the general price level since it would affect wealth, income, and consumption proportionately. However, in one respect inflation has a distorting influence—on income from interest. Inflation would appear to make holders of fixed-interest wealth worse off by eroding the purchasing value of their assets. Short-term interest rates, however, generally rise and fall in step with variations in inflation, and the interest rates on longer-term assets are believed to incorporate expectations of future inflation. Thus, investors may be partially or fully compensated for inflation in the form of higher interest payments.

In an inflationary environment, a portion of the nominal interest payment should be thought of as a repayment of principal, or amortization, required to maintain the real value of financial assets and not as fully equivalent to other forms of nominal income (Jump 1980). If the recipients of the income payments (creditors) understand this distinction between nominal and real interest income, they would not spend the inflation component of their interest income, using it instead to replenish the real value of their wealth. Thus, we might expect to see their reported rates of saving rise and fall with variations in price inflation. In contrast, net borrowers would have an inflation-induced net reduction in their debts and might react by increasing their consumption—reducing their saving. At the most aggregate level, the net effect of inflation on lenders and debtors should be a wash.

Historically, households have been net purchasers of debt instruments from business and government; any inflation-induced increases in saving of households should have been offset by inflation-induced reductions in saving by the business and government sectors.[10] However, beginning in 2000, the household sector became a net debtor in terms of directly held interest-bearing assets and liabilities, reflecting the growing concentration of wealth in housing and equities on the one hand and the rise of mortgage debt on the other. As a result, the household sector continued to be a net holder of interest-bearing debt only if indirect holdings through retirement accounts are included as part of household wealth.

A measure of the household saving rate adjusted for the inflation premium of reported interest income is shown in figure 2-3. The premium is computed by multiplying the rate of inflation by an estimate of household net interest-bearing wealth.[11] Interest-bearing wealth is defined as

10. For the economy as a whole, the inflation adjustment is of little consequence unless a country has large debts to the rest of the world.

11. The inflation rate is measured by the year-over-year change in the average of the fourth- and first-quarter values of the personal consumption expenditure deflator of the national accounts.

Figure 2-3. *Personal Saving Adjusted for Inflation, 1980–2010*

Percent of disposable income

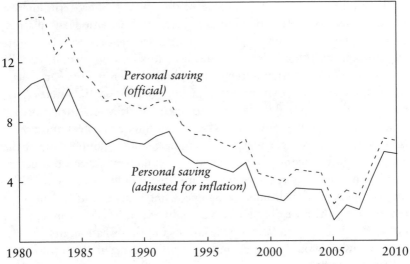

Sources: Bureau of Economic Analysis (2011a, table 2.1) and author's calculations.

deposits and credit market assets less credit market liabilities. The calculations for households include the interest-bearing assets and liabilities of noncorporate enterprises and assets held indirectly through pension plans, life insurance, personal trusts, and mutual funds (Perozek and Reinsdorf 2002). This inflation premium is subtracted from the reported saving rate to compute the underlying real rate. The adjustment was quite large in the 1970s, averaging nearly 4 percent of disposable income, but it fell steadily in subsequent decades and was only 0.1 percent in 2005–09. The decline was due to the slowing of inflation, the reduced importance of fixed-interest assets in household wealth holdings, and the growth of mortgage debt. Thus, lower inflation is a potentially important explanation for some of the reduction in the reported saving rate. There is, however, little empirical evidence on the effect of inflation on individuals' perceptions of their interest income and their saving behavior. Certainly, in international cases of extremely high inflation we can observe that investors avoid fixed-interest assets, and inflation is critical to understanding changes in saving behavior, but the effects of more moderate rates of inflation, such as experienced in the United States, are uncertain.

Broad Versus Narrow Saving Measures

Many analysts believe that the current definition of capital in the national accounts is too narrow. The origins of this discussion are related to the development of the national accounts during World War II and the immediate postwar period. The emphasis was on creating an integrated framework that would be useful in implementing the ideas of Keynesian economics on the origins of short-run business cycle fluctuations and tracing out the ramifications of changes in government spending, investment, and taxes. Within that framework, the concept of investment stressed the purchase of durable goods by businesses rather than the consumption purchases of households. It was well suited to measuring short-run changes in the demand side of the economy. However, over subsequent decades the emphasis has steadily shifted toward the importance of understanding the determinants of the supply side of the economy and its growth. That has spurred interest in a set of accounts that would include a broader range of capital, such as education, research and development, and other intangibles that have a strong influence on economic growth.[12] Within that system, the definition of investment changes to emphasize outlays that are designed to increase future production rather than consumption outlays that are used within the current period. Progress in implementing this broader framework for capital is limited primarily by concerns about developing objective measures of value that can be linked to observable market transactions.

This issue of the breadth of the definition of capital is important for two primary reasons. First, by expanding the range of capital inputs, the broader definition contributes to a more complete description of the production process and leaves less to be accounted for by a residual of unmeasured factors grouped under "multifactor productivity" or "technical change." Also, it has been argued that the narrow definition of capital leads to an inaccurate characterization of the United States as a low-saving and low-investment economy.[13] Instead, it is claimed that the United

---

12. A recent illustration of an expanded set of economic accounts is provided in Jorgenson, Landefeld, and Nordhaus (2006). Important antecedents are Kendrick (1961, 1976), Ruggles and Ruggles (1982), and Eisner (1989).

13. Prominent proponents of that perspective are Eisner (1991) and Lipsey and Kravis (1987).

States devotes an unusually high share of its income to purchases—such as consumer durables, research and development, and education—that are excluded from the definition of capital investment in the national accounts.

Consumer Durables

A defining feature of a capital good is that it provides a stream of services beyond the period of its purchase. Thus, home purchase is treated as an investment because it yields future housing services (rent). In contrast, restaurant meals are consumed immediately and are classified as consumption expenditures. However, consumer purchases of durable goods, which are similar to capital goods in that they provide a stream of services that last well beyond the period in which they are purchased, seem to fall in an intermediate category. Some, like the purchase of automobiles, are especially difficult because they are classified as investment if purchased by a business. Thus, some observers would prefer to classify the purchase of a durable good as an investment, remove it from consumption, and use a measure of the flow of services from past purchases as the measure of consumption. In effect, consumer durables would be treated in a fashion identical to that of owner-occupied housing. National accountants formerly pointed to the use of market rents as a firmer basis for the imputation of housing services, but today, equivalent information is available for automobiles and other consumer durables, because they can be leased for extended periods.

Although the Bureau of Economic Analysis (BEA) currently reports the purchase of durables as a consumer expenditure, it does provide estimates of the stock of consumer durables. That information is used in turn by the Federal Reserve to compute an alternative measure of saving in the flow of funds accounts that shifts the purchase of consumer durables from consumption to investment and imputes an estimate of the service flow back to consumption. However, the flow of funds does not include a full accounting of the service flow, as is done with homeownership: the flow of consumption services is simply equal to the depreciation of the capital stock, and there is no imputation of net income to the owners of the capital. The treatment of consumer durables as investment does increase household saving by 2 to 3 percent of disposable income, and it does dampen the volatility of saving over the business cycle; however, it has no significant effect on the extent of the secular deterioration in the rate (figure 2-4).

Figure 2-4. *Personal Saving and Consumer Durables, 1970–2010*

Percent of disposable income

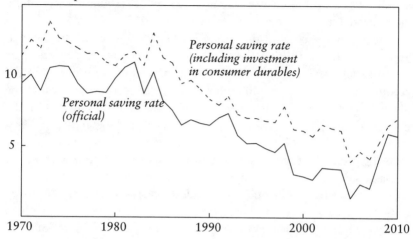

Sources: Board of Governors of the Federal Reserve (2011a) and author's calculations.

Research and Development

The importance of research and development (R&D) as a source of economic growth has long been recognized, and the failure to include it as a component of investment in the national accounts has been largely due to measurement problems.[14] R&D activities are difficult to value because the outputs are infrequently exchanged through markets and are often developed in house. Thus, they lack an observable price that can be used to aggregate investments of different vintages. In addition, it is difficult to measure their rate of depreciation (obsolescence). The issue became more critical in the 1990s, when advances in information technology emerged as a primary source of U.S. productivity growth, and the importance of the issue stimulated new research aimed at measuring its contribution to

14. In their work on the contribution of intangibles to economic growth, Corrado, Hulten, and Sichel (2005) went further and defined intangible capital to encompass computerized information, scientific and nonscientific R&D, advertizing and brand development, and firm-specific human capital. The authors argue that this broad measure of intangibles investment is roughly equal to investments in tangibles. However, there is less acceptance of defining some of these other elements as capital. Advertising, in particular, seems to be more related to obtaining a competitive advantage than to making an investment with benefits to future production.

economic growth. Progress has been made in creating a satellite account of the U.S. national accounts that develops the methodology for including R&D as a capital investment, and the new definitions are to be fully incorporated in the core national accounts in 2013.

Currently, the costs of producing R&D are included in the national accounts in the sense that the labor and capital costs are included as expenses. However, they are recorded as a consumption outlay in the accounts for government and nonprofit research institutions; within the business sector, the expenses are recorded as an intermediate cost in the production of other products rather than as a final expenditure. Thus, increases in business R&D are shown as raising business expenses and reducing profits. For the government and nonprofit components, the shift in classification from consumption to investment is similar to that for consumer durables and would have modest effects on the overall measure of GDP; however, moving business R&D from a current intermediate expense to investment would lead to an increase in the level of GDP equal to the value of the R&D investment. On the income side, business net income and the depreciation allowance would together increase by an equivalent amount. For government and nonprofit institutions, the change would raise investment and saving by matching amounts. Thus, the reclassification of R&D would raise the reported saving of business, government, and nonprofit research institutions. A detailed discussion of the effects of the classification change on reported GDP is provided in Okubo and others (2006).[15] R&D expenditures are to be included as a component of capital accumulation in the next revision of the national income accounts.

Expenditures on R&D are shown in the top panel of figure 2-5 as a percent of GDP. A distinction is also made between public and privately funded investments. Overall R&D investment has been a relatively stable 2.5 to 3 percent of GDP since 1960, but the publicly funded share has

15. The national accounts currently include a capital account for the non–R&D investments of government and private nonprofits (part of the household sector), but the imputation for capital services is limited to adding depreciation to consumption. In effect, when a zero rate of return is assumed, the services of all public capital are undervalued in the current system of national accounts. Several researchers have argued for changing the practice to include a net return for government capital (Jorgenson, Landefeld, and Nordhaus 2006). Perhaps in anticipation of this more general change but also to increase comparability with R&D funded by business, the R&D satellite account of BEA includes an imputed measure of the net return to publicly funded R&D.

Figure 2-5. *Investment in Research and Development*

Panel A.
Investment in research and development as a percent of adjusted GDP

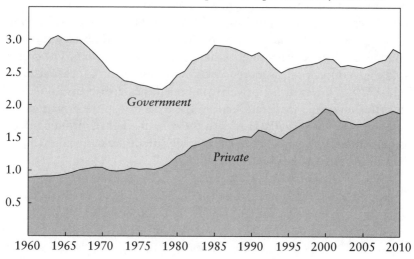

Panel B.
Net investment in research and development as a percent of adjusted GDP

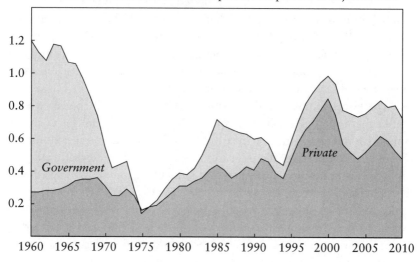

Sources: National Science Foundation (2010); Bureau of Economic Analysis (2011a); and author's calculations.

fallen steadily from about two-thirds in the 1960s to one-third today. Part of the reduction in the public share can be traced to the inflated size of the space program in the 1960s, when the United States was engaged in a program to reach the moon, but there has also been a shift toward greater emphasis on applied work with patents and commercial applications. The lower panel adjusts for depreciation and obsolescence and computes the increments to government and private saving. The decline in the government role is more marked and actually turns negative in the mid-1970s. However, the private component has grown over time, and its inclusion would moderate some of the reduction in the private saving rate since the early 1980s. However, the overall effect of including R&D is quite modest; it would raise the overall rate of net national saving by less than 1 percentage point.

Education

At present, expenditures on formal education are reported in the national accounts as consumption outlays of households and governments. There is widespread agreement that most of these expenditures should be recorded as investments rather than consumption because they provide a stream of benefits that extend far into the future. In addition, a large portion of the benefits have a monetary value and enhance workers' contribution to future output. It has been difficult, however, to develop quantitative measures of the value of education. In market economies, goods and services are valued by their prices, but the education embodied in a human being cannot be bought and sold. Hence there is no immediate measure of the value of an education.

The effort to measure the output of education has involved two different methodologies. The first approaches the issue from the cost side, similar to the factor-income measures of value added in other industries. From this perspective, the expenditures consist of the direct outlays of households and of governments' and students' forgone earnings during the education period. Estimates of the direct outlays are readily available, but measures of the forgone income would need to be imputed. Some pioneering work was done in Kendrick (1976) and extended by Eisner (1989), but it requires a number of improvised assumptions. It is not evident how education costs should be allocated between the learning component that contributes to future income and the portion that represents pure consumption. [16] Similarly, it is difficult to allocate faculty costs in higher education between teaching and research activities. The full integration of the investment component into the national accounts would also require the ability to cumulate the flows, account for depreciation, and provide a measure of the flow of services from the stock. These measurement problems are the principal reason that these expenditures are currently classified as consumption rather than investment.

The alternative methodology focuses on valuing the output, but because there is no immediate price, it is measured by the increment to future earnings that the investment can be expected to provide. Thus, Jorgenson and Fraumeni (1989) develops a measure of output that is equal to the present value of the returns. The authors measure the returns by comparing the earnings of individuals of similar age and gender but different levels of educational attainment. The contribution of education to nonmarket activities is measured by assuming an equalization of the marginal benefits of work and leisure.

In principle, the marginal costs of an education should approximate its marginal benefits, but in practice, the output-based measures of Jorgenson and Fraumeni are much larger than those based on the costs (Abraham 2010), perhaps because the risks associated with assessing the future value of an education lead individuals to invest too little, leaving the marginal returns well above the costs. But it is also difficult to measure the returns to learning allowing for an alternative view, that a major function of the education process is the simple sorting of individuals with different abilities (Spence 1973). At present there also is no agreement on a method for partitioning education expenditures between consumption and investment, or on appropriate measures of the value of the output and its rate of depreciation. Nor is there a means of distinguishing between education and research activities. Thus, we can provide only rough estimates of gross nominal outlays on education.

A simple measure of educational outlays over the period of 1970–2009 is presented in figure 2-6. Direct government and private expenditures on

16. Some studies of student time allocation during the college years suggest that remarkably few hours are spent on learning activities. The American Time Use Survey, for example, reports that the average college and university student spends little more than three hours a day on educational activities. These data are tabulated by the Bureau of Labor Statistics for the years 2005–09 and reported on its website at www. bls.gov/tus/charts/students.htm.

Figure 2-6. *Gross Investment in Education, 1970–2009*

Percent of adjusted national income

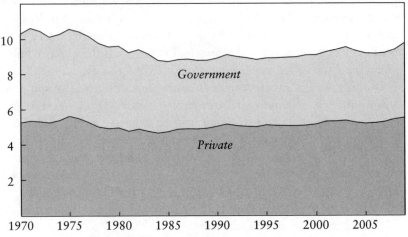

Sources: Bureau of Economic Analysis (2011a, tables 2.5.5 and 3.15.5) and author's calculations.

education are readily available in the national accounts, and they are augmented by a measure of forgone earnings.[17] Total education expenditures are large, but they are very stable within the range of 8.5 to 9 percent of adjusted GNI over the 1970–2009 period. Similarly, the allocation between public and private spending has been unchanging, averaging 5 and 3.5 percent of adjusted GNI, respectively. Within the private component, direct costs have slowly increased from 0.9 percent of GNI in the 1970s to 1.4 percent in the last decade, offset by a downward trend in the estimate of forgone earnings. It seems clear that reclassifying education as an investment rather than a consumption expense would significantly raise the measured rates of saving and investment; however, there is little indication that it would alter the overall trend because expenditures

17. The expenditure data are from tables 3.15.5 and 2.5.5 of the national income and product accounts. The number of employable students was obtained by using the unemployment and labor force participation rates for their age group. Forgone earnings are equal to the minimum wage for secondary school students. Post-secondary students are assumed to earn the average wage of workers in their age group. The estimates do not include business investment in worker training programs.

on education, both public and private, have been surprisingly constant shares of national income for more than forty years.

Sector Saving Measures

As illustrated in table 2-1, the U.S. national accounts make it possible to divide national saving into government and private components and further to partition private saving between the household and corporate sectors. The quality of the government saving data is quite high since they are obtained from budget data, and private saving is a residual measure. Only a few countries are able to produce measures of household and corporate saving because of the incomplete nature of corporate (or quasi-corporate) financial records.[18] As a residual affected by the estimation of almost all other income and expenditure items in the national accounts, household saving is often subject to large revisions—particularly for the latest years. In addition, the U.S. measures differ from those of many other countries in that saving is usually reported net of capital consumption allowances (depreciation).

There is significant controversy about the extent to which government, corporate, and household saving can be viewed as independent of one another. For example, many economists believe that corporations are simply agents of their owners and that stockholders see through the "corporate veil." Hence they will counteract any change in the corporation's retained earnings with adjustments in their own saving so as to leave private saving unaffected. Denison (1958) noted, for example, that private saving, the sum of corporate and household saving, was more stable than either of its components, suggesting that variations in the two components may offset each other.[19] It is largely an issue of short-run dynamics since both household wealth and private wealth are defined to include the net value of the corporate sector. As discussed more fully in later chapters, the choice between private and household saving as the appropriate behavioral concept has taken on added importance in recent

18. Quasi-corporations are enterprises that maintain separate financial records and behave as distinct economic units even though they do not have corporate status. In the United States, partnerships and sole proprietorships are included with households and are not broken out as separate economic units.

19. The issue has been explored empirically in major studies by Hendershott and Peek (1989), Poterba (1987), and Auerbach and Hassett (1999).

years because of substantial divergence in the trends of household and corporate saving in several countries.

An equal degree of debate has surrounded the validity of the distinction between private and government saving, in what has come to be known as Ricardian equivalence. Barro (1974) argued that citizens would internalize the debt and assets of government as their own. Hence any change in the public saving balance would be offset by adjustments to private saving. If true, it implies that a tax cut financed by higher borrowing would have no impact on increasing aggregate demand because consumers would save the tax cut to pay the future tax increases. The relevance of the alternative sector saving concepts is examined in greater detail in the following chapter on saving behavior.

Conclusion

The coexistence of a large decline in measured rates of saving and a substantial rise in the wealth-income ratio is a puzzling aspect of U.S. economic performance over the past quarter-century. It has led a substantial number of economists to be skeptical of the official measures and to suggest various alternatives. The most common proposal is to redefine saving to be equal to the change in wealth. However, the argument of this chapter has been that these are two distinct concepts that are both useful, but in different contexts. They represent separate portions of an integrated set of economic accounts that include both income statements and balance sheets. The change in wealth is composed of two separate components, saving and valuation changes. Saving is defined by the portion of current production that is used to provide for additions to wealth, and it is largely determined by explicit decisions of individual agents. Valuation changes, in contrast, are driven by changes in markets and are largely beyond the control of the individual.

This chapter also considers proposals to make various other adjustments to the definition of saving. Many of those proposals have considerable conceptual appeal, and some have been incorporated in revisions to the national accounts—for example, those regarding computer software and R&D. The effects of those proposals over the 1970–2010 period are shown in table 2-2. The inclusion of consumer durables would significantly change the cyclical pattern of saving, but there would be only a limited effect on the trend. The adjustment for inflation would offset much of the observed secular saving decline, but there is very little

Table 2-2. *Summary of Potential Adjustments to Household Saving*
Percent of disposable income

Item	1970–79	1980–89	1990–99	2000–07	2008–10
Household saving	9.6	8.6	5.5	2.8	5.3
Potential adjustment to household saving					
Consumer durables	2.5	2.2	1.9	2.8	0.9
Inflation adjustment	3.7	2.8	1.5	0.4	0.2
Realized capital gains	3.3	4.9	4.3	6.3	4.4
Real capital gains	8.3	11.9	21.8	14.4	–32.2
Wealth-income ratio	4.1	4.3	4.8	5.5	4.5

Sources: Bureau of Economic Analysis (2011a); Board of Governors of the Federal Reserve (2011a); and author's estimates. The estimates of realized capital gains were obtained from Treasury data available in Congressional Budget Office (2011, table 4.3).

research about the extent to which households are actually aware of the implications of variations in the inflation rate and incorporate it into their decisionmaking. Other suggestions, such as the inclusion of investments in education, are limited by measurement problems that make it difficult to define output or to draw a firm line between consumption and investment. However, most of the suggested changes would have little impact on the trend of declining private and national saving.

CHAPTER THREE

Why Don't
Americans Save?

The effort to explain the decline in saving has generated a large volume of research over the past several decades. Despite that effort, a consensus on the reasons for the falloff has yet to emerge. As shown in chapter 2, problems of measurement do not appear to be a sufficient explanation, and most researchers would agree that the reduced rate of saving is a real phenomenon. The theoretical emphasis on life-cycle theories of consumer behavior led to an initial focus on demographic change and the aging of the U.S. population, but the reduced saving preceded the retirement of the baby boom generation by several decades and occurred while an unusually high proportion of American workers were in their prime saving years. Others have suggested that the expansion of government income and health care programs targeting the elderly may have reduced individuals' perception of the need to save for retirement (Gokhale, Kotlikoff, and Sabelhaus 1996). Again, however, timing is a problem: most of the changes in those programs date back to the 1960s or even earlier and do not seem to be closely tied to the fall in saving rates during the late 1980s and 1990s. Changes in financial markets may also have contributed by lessening financial constraints and thereby enabling households to increase their borrowing, which may have had the effect of both reducing their actual saving and reducing their motivation to save as a precautionary measure.

Perhaps the most popular current explanation is based on a "wealth effect," whereby the strong increase in household net worth over the past three decades reduced the need to save and led households to increase their spending relative to current income. Yet while a negative association between the saving rate and the wealth-income ratio seems evident in the aggregate data (see chapter 2, figure 2-1), questions have also been raised about its timing: the initial years of reduced saving preceded episodes of large capital gains, and there are many short-run variations in wealth that do not appear to lead to changes in saving. There also are differences between the emphasis placed on valuation gains in housing and that placed on gains in corporate equities.

In addition to a plethora of uncertain explanations for the reduced saving, we do not know whose saving has fallen or whether the decline is universal or limited to a few key household groups. While much of the national discussion refers to reduced rates of saving by the average household, the aggregate data actually reflect the saving out of the average dollar. Given the extreme skewness of the income distribution, it is possible that the reduced saving (increased consumption) reflects the behavior of a few very rich households with the largest wealth gains. It would be helpful to know, for example, whether the changes in asset prices actually affect the consumption of the asset holders or if changes in asset prices and aggregate consumption are simply driven by common factors.

In the following sections, the decline in the saving rate is examined from both a macro- and a microeconomic perspective. The aggregate analysis relies heavily on data drawn from the national income and flow of funds accounts. It provides increased detail about the reduction in the saving rate, its relationship to changes in the composition of household wealth, and the influence of wealth changes on consumption and saving. (An international comparison of changes in saving within other countries, another important source of insight, is taken up in a separate chapter.) The microeconomic perspective, which makes use of several surveys on household wealth accumulation over the past quarter-century, is directed at two major issues. First, can the survey data provide any insight into whose saving has declined? Second, what are the consequences of reduced saving at the individual level? For example, has it adversely affected individuals' preparations for retirement?

A Life-Cycle Perspective

The life-cycle model (Modigliani and Brumberg 1954) has become the standard framework for thinking about consumption behavior. While the literature is concerned primarily with the determinants of consumption, it also translates into direct implications for saving behavior. In its simplest form, the life-cycle model argues that individuals will smooth consumption over their lifetime given expected lifetime resources. The theory leads to the prediction that individuals will exhibit a saving rate that rises with income during their work life and declines and turns negative during retirement. The aggregate saving rate, therefore, depends critically on the relative size of different age cohorts in the population. Unfortunately, this basic model offers limited insight into recent changes in saving within the United States since there has been no significant change in the age structure of the population. However, contributions to the consumption literature in recent years have expanded the model to include other influences on consumption and saving. An extensive survey is provided in Browning and Lusardi (1996). The additions include evaluation of the role of uncertainty with respect to future income and life span (encouraging precautionary saving), liquidity constraints, and the desire to leave bequests (or dynastic savings).[1]

The life-cycle model has also been extended to take more explicit account of the role of accumulated wealth at various stages of life and the effect of unanticipated changes in the value of that wealth on consumption. It suggests that while predictable changes in asset prices should have little or no effect, unexpected changes should generate a change in planned consumption. The simplest formulation of that model suggests that the marginal propensity to spend out of different types of wealth should be a uniform small number. In practice, however, not all forms of wealth are equally liquid; the response may vary depending on the changes in the prices of specific components of wealth. The life-cycle model is a useful framework, but its breadth also implies that it does not rule out many potential explanations for reduced saving.

The Composition of Saving

The unprecedented magnitude of the fall in household saving is very evident in figure 3-1. The personal saving rate fell from an average of 8.6 percent of national income in the 1980s to 2.8 percent in 2000–07 before

---

1. Recent references on liquidity-constrained consumption behavior include Zeldes (1989) and Deaton (1991). Researchers emphasizing the importance of precautionary saving and doubting the empirical importance of the life-cycle theory include Deaton (1992), Carroll (1997, 2001) and Carroll and Samwick (1997).

Figure 3-1. *Personal and Private Saving as a Percent of National Income*

Percent

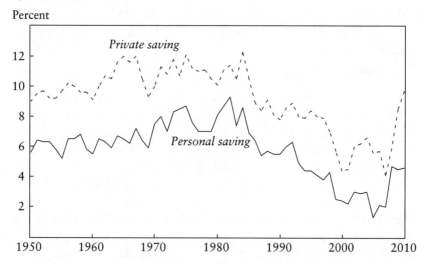

Sources: Bureau of Economic Analysis (2011a, tables 1.7.5, 2.1, and 5.1) and author's calculations.

rebounding to 5.5 percent during the financial crisis in 2008–10.[2] Prior to the 1980s, the saving rate had actually shown evidence of a modest upward trend with very limited annual fluctuations. The broader measure of private saving, which includes corporate retained earnings, indicates a very similar pattern. Corporate saving fell as a share of national income in the 1980s, but it was not part of the decline of the past two decades.[3] Thus, most of the following discussion focuses on household saving. There are, however, substantial differences in the liquidity of different forms of saving, and it can be useful to distinguish among retirement saving accounts, home equity, and other more marketable forms

2. In the chart, personal saving is scaled by national income to compare with private saving, but it is more frequently reported as a percent of household disposable income. The latter presentation slightly amplifies the magnitude of the fall in the saving rate because household disposable income has become a larger share of national income.

3. An alternative perspective that focuses on consumption rather than saving was provided in figure 1-1 in chapter 1. The share of GDP devoted to private consumption fluctuated within a narrow range in the period of 1951–80, but it has increased by 8 to 10 percent of GDP over the past thirty years.

of household saving. Also, individual households often have little or no knowledge of the status of their pension funds, and distinguishing between saving within retirement accounts and other forms of saving facilitates the comparison with estimates based on household surveys.

Retirement Saving

In many cases, saving within retirement accounts has a contractual element in that individual contributors are allowed to exert only limited control over their investment in the short run, and often they have a very imprecise knowledge of the accrued value.[4] There are three basic forms of retirement accounts: defined benefit, defined contribution, and individual retirement accounts. With the employer-sponsored defined benefit account, which dominated for several decades after World War II, the employee is promised an annual retirement benefit based on years of service, and it is the responsibility of the employer to manage the fund and finance the future benefit payments through a combination of contributions and investment earnings. Concerns about the credibility of employers' commitment to fulfilling their obligations and greater ease in transferring funds when workers change jobs has led to a shift toward defined contribution accounts, in which both employers and employees make contributions. A defined contribution account is owned by the employee, and the ultimate benefit amount depends on the amounts contributed and the return on the investment. The employee can receive the benefit in either a lump sum or an annual annuity. The crucial distinction between these two forms of retirement accounts revolves around the question of who bears the risk of fluctuations in the rate of return: in a defined benefit plan, the employer bears the risk; in a defined contribution plan, the employee does. However, defined benefit plans are not guaranteed against corporate bankruptcy, and even though these plans are partially insured by the government, individuals often lose major portions of their accrued benefits. Individual retirement accounts (IRAs) are a form of defined contribution plan, but they are independent of any employer relationship. Today, most of the contributions into IRAs are the result of employee transfers of balances (rollovers) from employer-provided

---

4. Because workers frequently have incomplete knowledge of the status of their retirement accounts, investments in such accounts are often excluded from household surveys of wealth holdings.

programs upon termination of a job. The capital income within all three of these types of retirement accounts is generally exempt from personal income taxation, but funds are subject to a penalty if they are withdrawn before the employee reaches a specified age.

The activities of the employer-sponsored pension plans are assigned to the household sector in the national accounts: employer contributions to the accounts are part of workers' compensation, and the investment earnings of the funds are part of household capital income. The saving within these accounts—defined as contributions plus investment earnings, less benefit payments and any administrative charges—represents a substantial portion of household saving and wealth. It also has a large demographic component: it rises initially, fueled by contributions and investment income with a relatively minor benefit outflow, but as the covered workforce ages, benefit payments rise and the net inflow begins to level out and ultimately turns negative.

The proportion of workers who participate in an employer-provided pension program has remained very stable at about half of the workforce over the past fifty years, but household surveys indicate that the proportion of workers participating in a plan peaked around 2000 and has been slowly receding in subsequent years. By imposing stricter regulation and funding requirements, the Employee Retirement Income Security Act (ERISA), passed in 1974, encouraged employers to shift away from defined benefit plans to defined contribution plans. In addition, defined contributions are more attractive to workers who are likely to change jobs in the middle of their careers. Defined benefit plans may be very back loaded, and the value of a pension early in an individual's career may be very small. The number of workers in primary defined contribution plans surpassed those in defined benefit plans in the mid-1990s; by 2010, 60 to 65 percent of the assets of private sector pension plans were in defined contribution plans. Some of the remaining defined benefit plans have also been converted to cash balance plans that share many of the characteristics of defined contribution plans.[5] The federal government likewise converted to a defined contribution system for workers hired after 1983. Defined benefit plans remain popular within the state and

5. Under a defined benefit plan, benefits accrue at an accelerated rate in the years just prior to retirement. In contrast, benefits in the cash balance plan accrue at a more uniform rate over a worker's career with a contribution proportionate to the annual salary and a guaranteed yield. The transferable balance will generally be higher for younger workers but lower at normal retirement.

local government sector, but numerous abuses surfaced in the aftermath of the 2008–09 financial crisis.

The question of whether pension funds constitute a net addition to household wealth has been a subject of considerable debate and research. In the simplest life-cycle model, workers save only for retirement, and changing the form of their current compensation from wages to contributions to a pension plan should have no effect on their consumption. That is, the pension plan is doing nothing that individuals could not do for themselves, and participation in formal pension plans may simply lead individual to reduce other forms of saving. In practice, however, the income earned within the accounts receives favorable tax treatment that may affect saving decisions, and for households that face liquidity constraints, the plans may be a form of forced saving. It is also argued that some workers may be overly myopic or lack the knowledge to successfully invest in financial markets, and for them pension plans offer a more disciplined form of saving with superior management and higher rates of return. Thus, the degree of substitutability between pension and nonpension wealth is not easily determined.

On balance, the existing research suggests that large portions of existing pension wealth represent a reallocation of funds out of less tax-preferred assets rather than a net addition to saving. The issue was first raised in Feldstein (1974) with respect to the effects of Social Security on private saving, but the lack of major variation in the parameters of the system has limited the ability to measure its effect. Therefore, most recent research has centered on substitution between private pensions and other saving. Gale (2005) provides a recent summary of the research literature, which the author characterizes as suggesting a high degree of substitution of pension accounts with other forms of saving—in the neighborhood of 50 percent or more. Similar results are reported in Engelhardt and Kumar (2007), but the authors argued that the offset is concentrated among high-wealth households, which are presumably more sensitive to the tax considerations. Burtless and Toder (2010) shows that the tax advantage of pension accounts has declined over time due to the increasingly favorable tax treatment of other forms of capital income earned outside of pension funds.

The significance of retirement saving programs is highlighted in table 3-1 by separating the flow of household saving, as a share of disposable income, between retirement and nonretirement saving. Retirement saving is further segmented into the various types of pension accounts and individual

Table 3-1. *Household Saving and Its Components, 1952–2010*

Percent of household disposable income (period average)

Category	1970– 79	1980– 89	1990– 99	2000– 07	2008– 10
Household saving (NIPA)	9.6	8.6	5.5	2.8	5.3
Retirement saving[a]	4.4	7.3	6.1	5.3	3.0
Pension reserves	4.2	5.9	4.1	3.2	1.5
Individual retirement accounts	0.1	1.4	2.0	2.1	1.5
Other saving	5.2	1.3	–0.6	–2.5	2.3
Pension fund reserve accumulation	4.2	5.9	4.1	3.2	1.5
Public employee plans	0.4	0.8	0.8	0.6	0.7
Life insurance companies	0.8	1.5	1.4	1.7	0.6
Private pension funds	2.1	2.2	0.8	0.4	0.3
Defined benefit		0.3	-0.1	-0.6	-0.5
Defined contribution		1.1	0.9	1.0	0.8
Statistical discrepancy					
Household saving (NIPA)	9.6	8.6	5.5	2.8	5.3
Household saving (FFA)	11.3	10.9	6.5	1.6	5.9
NIPA-FFA (discrepancy)	–1.7	–2.3	–1.0	1.3	–0.6

Sources: Bureau of Economic Analysis (2011a); Board of Governors of the Federal Reserve (2011a); and author's calculations.

a. Retirement saving data are taken from the flow of funds accounts.

retirement accounts. Net pension fund accumulation was a slowly rising share of total household saving in the years up to the 1980s, when the pension system was still maturing, and it reached a peak of about 6 percent of disposable income in the mid-1980s. Since then, it has steadily fallen as a percent of disposable income, averaging only 2 percent of income in 2005–09. The inflow of funds to IRAs grew substantially during the 1980s and was a stable 2 percent of income until the financial crisis; recent estimates are still quite preliminary. Total retirement saving peaked at about 7 percent of disposable income in the 1980s and fell to 5 percent in the 2000s. It dropped very sharply during the financial crisis. Meanwhile, nonretirement saving fell sharply in the 1980s and turned negative after 1995. It is the category that shows the largest increase in 2010.

A more disaggregate view of the different types of retirement accounts is shown in the middle portion of table 3-1. Net saving within public employee funds is published in the national accounts, but the accumulation of funds within private sector pension funds, those managed by life insurance companies, and IRAs are not specifically identified. In constructing the table, data on the reserve accumulation of private pension and life insurance funds and IRAs are taken from the flow of funds accounts. Because of the exclusion of capital gains and losses, saving within pension programs can be quite different from the overall change in pension reserves. For example, large capital gains on equities in the late 1990s pushed some of the defined benefit plans into "overfunded" status, which enabled employers to reduce their contributions.[6] It is also notable that private defined benefit plans have had a negative net saving flow since the mid-1980s, consistent with their declining role. The overall rate of contribution into the pension system has been stable since the mid-1970s, however, and the big change is in the large increase in the outflow of benefits as the plans mature. There has been no reduction of pension saving within life insurance companies, but many of those accounts reflect the transfer of funds from other pension plans to finance retirement annuities. A large portion of the funds that flow into IRAs today are the result of the rollover of employer-provided pension accounts occasioned by job terminations.[7] In 2010, IRAs accounted for $4.5 trillion in household wealth, while formal pensions accounted for $13 trillion.

Other Saving

If the falloff in saving is dated to begin in the 1980s, the largest drop has been in nonretirement saving, which fell to zero in the late 1980s and turned sharply negative in the late 1990s. It also saw the largest increase in the aftermath of the financial crisis. We can be relatively confident that the saving decline is not just a statistical illusion. While the flow of funds accounts (FFA) measure of household saving is more volatile than that of the national income and product accounts (NIPAs), it shows a very similar pattern of deterioration. Because of a change in sign of the statistical discrepancy, the FFA measure actually indicates an even larger drop in the rate of nonretirement saving in the years after 1980.

6. In effect, defined benefit retirement accounts function like target savers in that capital gains induce a negative offset in saving through a reduction in employer contributions.

7. A summary of the research on the disposition of lump-sum distributions and some recent results are available in Verma and Lichtenstein (2006).

Despite concerns about the employer-based pension system, it is evident that the bulk of the decline in saving lies largely outside of pension accounts. While pension saving has fallen over the past thirty years, it is the result of a maturing of the system as it approaches an equilibrium balance of beneficiaries and contributors. The role of pensions in the reduced rate of overall saving would be even less if there was significant substitution between the pension and nonpension saving since, as noted by Burtless and Toder (2010), pension accounts have less favorable tax treatment than in the past.

Survey-Based Saving Measures

The continuing controversy over the source of the fall in the saving rate is due primarily to the difficulty of obtaining meaningful measures of saving at the individual household level. Discriminating among many of the competing hypotheses requires the ability to observe the saving of different types of households. That is especially true for explanations that attribute the decline to changes in the composition of households by age (demographics), homeownership, prior wealth accumulation, or access to credit. Bosworth, Burtless, and Sabelhaus (1991) used several micro-surveys of household saving to examine the causes of the early decline in saving rates during the 1980s. The authors aligned the survey-based estimates of saving with aggregate concepts of the national accounts. Although they found some of the drop in the saving rate concentrated among older persons, they concluded that it was a rather general phenomenon that affected a large number of households.

Since that time, there has been a large increase in data from household-level surveys. Unfortunately, the quality of the additional information on saving is disappointingly low, and the pattern of overall change provided by the survey-based estimates does not correspond with that of the national accounts. A measure of saving can be constructed from the surveys using two different methods. The first defines saving as after-tax income minus consumption. It mirrors the approach of the national accounts, but at the level of the individual consumer. This is the method used in the Consumer Expenditure Survey (CEX), which has been conducted on an ongoing basis since the early 1980s to provide up-to-date information on the composition of consumers' expenditures. The second method is based on obtaining information on a household's wealth holdings at two points in time and computing saving as the change in wealth, exclusive of capital gains and losses. It was first employed in the 1962–63 Survey of Changes in Family Finances (SCFF),[8] and it has been a part of the Panel Study of Income Dynamics (PSID) since 1984 and the Health and Retirement Survey (HRS) of older households since 1992.

The saving rate measures constructed from the survey data differ in several respects from the national accounts concepts. First and most important, they exclude saving within pension funds because very little information is available on pension balances at the household level. Within the CEX, employer contributions to pension accounts and the earnings on those accounts are not included as part of a household's reported income, and benefits are included as part of income rather than a shift out of pension assets. When saving is constructed from the change in household wealth holdings, as in the PSID and HRS, households also have limited information on the status of their pension accounts. Second, the surveys differ from the national accounts in their treatment of health expenditures and housing. The national accounts impute third-party payments for health care as an element of both income and expenditures. In contrast, the surveys exclude third-party payments from both income and consumption. These offsetting adjustments to income and consumption, however, result in little or no change in the estimate of saving. Third, the national accounts treat homeownership as a business, imputing an estimate of the rental value to consumption and adding that value less interest, taxes, depreciation, and maintenance costs to income. Again, this treatment of housing has little impact on saving as long as the residual of net rental income is small.

Consumer Expenditure Survey

Versions of the CEX have been conducted on a periodic basis for more than a century to obtain the expenditure weights or market basket used to construct the consumer price index. It has been reported on a continuous basis since 1980 with annual publication of the microdata files. Households are asked to report their income and consumption expenditures within a detailed set of categories. Saving can be computed as after-tax income minus consumption. Unfortunately, the estimates of saving are not credible, and the pattern of change bears little resemblance to that of the national accounts. In fact, the saving rate obtained from the CEX

8. Projector (1968).

rises dramatically from 3 percent in 1992 to 21 percent of income in 2009 (panel A of figure 3-2), a sharp contrast with the macroeconomic evidence of a falling trend.

The CEX survey is moderately successful in obtaining estimates of income, but respondents have great difficulty recalling the details of their consumption expenditures.[9] That difficulty is reflected in the steady deterioration in the estimate of consumption spending in the CEX. That pattern is highlighted in table 3-2, which is drawn from a recent study of the Bureau of Labor Statistics (Garner, McClelland, and Passero 2009). Over a fifteen-year period, the ratio of total consumer spending in the survey to that of the national accounts fell from 67 percent in 1992 to 59 percent in 2007. There are significant definitional differences in some categories; nevertheless, when the comparison is limited to very comparable groups, the decline in the ratio is still large—from 86 to 81 percent. The one exception was housing: the survey measure of expenditures slightly exceeds that of the national accounts.[10] An alternative perspective is provided in the lower panel of figure 3-2, which reports indexes of the growth in income and expenditures in the CEX and the national accounts for the period of 1992–2010. In this comparison, it is clear that the survey measure of consumer expenditures has grown much more slowly than that of the national accounts, presumably because the CEX is missing progressively larger portions of consumer spending.[11]

Panel Survey of Income Dynamics

The PSID is a longitudinal survey that began collecting information on household wealth in 1984. Households were reinterviewed about their wealth in 1989, 1994, 1999, and every two years thereafter. The

9. The definitions of disposable income and consumer spending are not exactly equivalent in the survey and the national accounts, but those differences play a minor role. In 2004, the CEX began to incorporate imputations in the measure of average income. In previous years, average income is based on data from complete-income reporters.

10. The two sources produce dramatic differences in the composition of consumer spending. Thus, the expenditure weights of the CPI are much different from the shares of consumer spending in the national accounts.

11. Some early comparisons of CEX and NIPA data attributed the discrepancies to definitional differences, and researchers proceeded in the belief that the ratio of the two measures would remain stable (Slesnick 1992; Attanasio 1998). However, later research by Garner, McClelland, and Passero showed those assumptions not to be true.

Figure 3-2. *Saving Trends in the Consumer Expenditure Survey*[a]

Panel A. Household saving rate, 1992–2010

Percent of disposable income

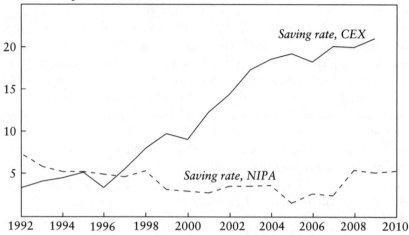

Panel B. Income and consumption, 1992–2010

Index (1992 = 100)

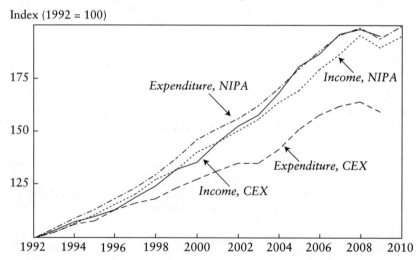

Sources: Bureau of Economic Analysis (2011a, table 2.1) and Bureau of Labor Statistics (2011).
  a. The saving rate from the Consumer Expenditure Survey is computed as 1 minus {(average annual expenditures less pension and Social Security contributions) divided by (after-tax income less pension and Social Security contributions)}.

Table 3-2. *Summary Comparison of Consumer Expenditures and Personal Consumption Expenditures, 1992–2007*
Percent of personal consumption expenditures

Item	1992	1997	2002	2007
All items	67.4	64.7	60.6	59.1
Comparable items	86.1	84.7	82.0	81.0
Housing	113.6	115.0	113.8	118.8
Comparable less housing	73.4	70.3	66.3	62.5
All items less housing	57.3	54.1	49.6	46.8

Source: Garner, McClelland, and Passero (2009, table 1).

longitudinal dimension of the PSID can be used to compute a measure of saving at the individual household level by calculating the difference in the balance for assets that are not subject to valuation changes (deposits, bonds, and loans) and using a specific question about purchases less sales to measure saving in those assets that are subject to price changes (equities, real estate, and own businesses).[12] Thus, the estimate of saving excludes unrealized capital gains and losses. An appealing aspect of the PSID is that it provides estimates of wealth and saving for a representative sample of U.S. households over the full interval of the decline in saving from the mid-1980s to the present.

Unfortunately, the PSID estimates of saving encounter measurement problems nearly as severe as those encountered with the CEX. To begin, the panel appears to under-represent high-wealth families and the estimates of wealth holdings are based on answers to questions about wealth in only eight broad categories. In contrast, the Survey of Consumer Finance (SCF), which is considered to be the premier source of information on wealth holdings, uses a special sampling frame that oversamples high-wealth households and includes a highly detailed set of questions about wealth holdings. The PSID yields distributions of wealth, however, that look remarkably similar to those of the SCF for the lower 95 percent of the wealth distribution (figure 3-3). Yet, because 60 percent of all wealth is in the top fifth percentile, the PSID yields an estimate of average wealth holdings that is much too low. While it may

12. This framework is explained in Juster and others (2006).

Figure 3-3. *Mean Household Wealth by Uniform Survey of Consumer Finance Decile, 1983–2007*[a]

Thousands of dollars

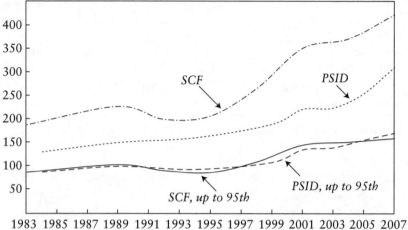

Sources: Panel Study of Income Dynamics (2011) data for 1983–2007; Board of Governors of the Federal Reserve (2010) Survey of Consumer Finance data for 1983–2007; and author's estimates.

a. Results are shown for the entire wealth distribution as well as for only those households whose wealth holdings fall below the 95th wealth percentile. Percentile breaks are determined in the Survey of Consumer Finances and applied to both surveys.

be representative of the average (median) family, it is not representative of the average dollar of wealth.

A second problem emerges with the computation of the change in wealth and the estimate of saving exclusive of valuation changes. The responses to the wealth questions include substantial measurement error, but because the error is largely random, the estimates of mean wealth in various socioeconomic groups are similar to those of the SCF. The differencing of an already noisy series (wealth), however, leads to a measure with a very high noise-to-signal ratio.[13] The result is relatively unstable

13. Due to funding shortages, the PSID has devoted only a small amount of resources to post-interview edits. An informal analysis of the wealth measures across waves of the survey reveals a substantial number of cases in which entry errors appear to have severely distorted the estimates, within an even more extreme effect on the changes. I interpret wealth estimates that differ from estimates for prior and later years by orders of magnitude to be entry errors rather than response errors.

Table 3-3. *Components of Saving and Wealth Accumulation in the Panel Study of Income Dynamics, 1984-2009*

Percent of income[a]

	Wealth-income ratio (1)	Wealth accumulation (2)	Total saving (3)	Equity-type assets (4)	Housing equity (5)	Fixed-price assets (6)	Median saving (7)
				Saving components			
Period							
1984–89	3.1	15.4	6.7	4.2	2.6	–0.2	2.6
1989–94	3.3	10.1	8.3	5.9	2.5	–0.1	1.6
1994–99	3.7	23.7	10.2	3.4	2.4	4.4	2.4
1999–01	3.8	16.8	10.0	2.1	4.0	3.9	1.7
2001–03	4.0	16.6	6.6	2.0	3.6	0.9	0.8
2003–05	4.3	40.0	16.1	2.8	5.9	7.4	1.0
2005–07	4.9	46.0	9.4	0.0	2.4	3.9	1.4
2007–09	3.6	–35.4	6.4	0.0	0.0	0.0	0.4

Sources: Panel Study of Income Dynamics (2011) and author's calculations. See Bosworth and Smart (2009) for details.

a. Except wealth-income ratio.

estimates of mean saving rates and little evidence of a secular decline. As shown in column 1 of table 3-3, the PSID does correspond with the flow of funds in showing a substantial rise in the wealth-income ratio after 1990, but it does not reflect the sustained drop in saving in column 3.[14] The lack of evidence of reduced saving cannot be attributed to any one component of saving. The median saving rate is more consistent with the notion of a secular decline, but given the skewed distribution of saving across income classes, it cannot be assumed to be representative of the average dollar of saving.

However, the tabulation of household wealth in the PSID by major socioeconomic group, as in table 3-4, clearly indicates the breadth of the increase in wealth holdings across a wide range of different types of

14. The PSID reports income only on a before-tax basis, but, unlike with the CEX, an estimate of after-tax income is not required to compute the measure of saving. Before-tax family income is used to scale all of the estimates of wealth, the change in wealth, and saving. The saving rates are computed as ratios of the means of saving and income.

Table 3-4. *Wealth-Income Ratio in the Panel Study of Income Dynamics, by Selected Characteristics*[a]

Characteristic	1984–89	1989–94	1994–99	1999–2001	2001–03	2003–05	2005–07	Change (1984–2007)
Full sample	3.1	3.7	3.9	4.0	4.1	4.2	4.9	1.8
Age of head								
25–39	1.7	1.7	2.0	1.6	1.9	2.1	1.7	0.1
40–49	3.6	3.3	2.7	2.9	3.1	3.2	3.9	0.3
50–59	4.2	4.4	5.9	4.3	4.5	4.2	5.2	1.1
60–69	5.5	6.7	7.0	7.5	7.5	7.6	8.4	2.9
70 and over	6.7	7.6	7.0	7.7	10.3	11.0	11.4	4.8
Education of head								
No high school degree	2.6	3.5	3.3	3.0	2.8	2.5	2.8	0.2
High school degree	2.6	3.2	4.1	4.0	3.7	3.5	4.2	1.6
Some college	3.3	2.9	3.2	3.5	3.6	4.0	4.5	1.2
College degree	3.8	4.7	4.4	4.5	4.8	4.9	5.8	2.0
More than college degree	3.2	3.9	4.2	4.4	5.4	5.8	6.3	3.1
Homeownership								
No	0.9	1.2	1.2	1.1	1.1	1.1	1.1	0.2
Yes	3.8	4.2	4.4	4.5	4.8	4.9	5.7	1.9
Business or farm ownership								
No	2.3	2.9	3.3	3.3	3.5	3.6	3.9	1.7
Yes	6.3	6.3	6.3	6.8	7.3	7.2	9.4	3.1

Sources: Panel Survey of Income Dynamics (2011) and author's calculations.
a. Wealth is an average of beginning and end of period surveys.

households. It reports the average wealth-income ratio within various groups over the twenty years that encompass the period of a downward trend in saving. There is a significant rise in wealth relative to income in all groups, but its magnitude rises with age and education (a proxy for income) and for homeowners and those owning a business. That pattern of change does not obviously fit arguments that the aged or any specific age cohort was a major source of reduced saving. Large reductions in saving within a specific group would be expected to result in a smaller-than-average increase in the wealth-income ratio.[15]

The inability to derive reliable measures of saving from the household surveys is a major setback in efforts to identify the sources of the fall in the saving rate. It also contrasts with earlier work in Bosworth, Burtless, and Sabelhaus (1991), where the authors were able to find a correspondence between changes in the household saving rate of the national accounts and the measures derived from several surveys extending back into the 1960s. Some researchers have attempted to adjust the microsurvey data to account for the measurement differences. Parker, for example, multiplied the individual household measures of expenditures on services and nondurable goods in the CEX by the ratio of the national accounts estimate to the corresponding total in the survey (Parker 2000). In effect, he assumed that the discrepancy is distributed across all households in proportion to their reported consumption.[16] Parker's data ended with 1994, and given the subsequent growth in the discrepancy, the adjustment has become very large, with no obvious reason for believing that it is proportionate to the reported levels of household consumption.

Accounting for the Saving Decline

In an extensive survey of the research literature, Browning and Lusardi identified as many as eleven potential reasons for the downward trend in rates of saving (Browning and Lusardi 1996). With the passage of time and a continuing decline, it is worth reviewing some of the most prevalent explanations, which include changes in the age distribution of the population (demography), capital gains/losses, increased annuitization of wealth, and improved access to credit.

15. The data also were arrayed by birth cohort over the period of 1984–2007. However, the cohort perspective showed the same pattern of rising or stable wealth-income ratios for successive cohorts. The sample was also restricted to a subset of continuously surveyed households that responded in all of the individual waves, but there was no appreciable effect on the pattern of wealth change.

16. The actual procedures are more complex as Parker first imputed the consumption estimates from the CEX to the PSID and then adjusted to the national accounts control. See pages 337–38 of Parker (2000).

Demography

The life-cycle hypothesis argues that retirement is a primary motive for saving. Thus, an individual's saving is expected to show a humped distribution over his or her life, and the aggregate saving rate should rise when higher percentages of the population are of working age and fall when the proportion that is young or aged increases. However, because the age distribution of the population changes very slowly over time, it has been difficult at the macroeconomic level to separate the effect of aging from other trend-dominated influences. Researchers have had some success with combining the data from a set of countries with divergent demographic trends and assuming that the marginal effects are the same across the set, but the results are highly dependent on the choice of countries (Hüfner and Koske 2010). The aggregate comparisons do make clear that very little aging has occurred in the United States relative to that in other industrialized countries. As shown in figure 3-4, the rise in the aged dependency rate (persons aged 65 and over as a percent of those aged 15–65) actually slowed after 1980, and it will accelerate in 2010–20. For most of the prior period, the baby boom generation was moving through its peak earning years, when rates of saving would be expected to be unusually high. In fact, a 1991 study (Auerbach, Cai, and Kotlikoff 1991) predicted that the maturing of the baby boomers would raise the saving rate. The degree of aging in the United States is especially modest compared with that in Japan and Western Europe (figure 3-4).[17] Thus, it is implausible that the small observed changes in the age distribution could account for the magnitude and speed of the observed drop in the saving rate. Instead, the potential effects of demographic change in the United States are largely in the future, when the baby boomers will be transitioning into retirement.

An alternative perspective on demographic influences emphasizes cohort effects in which the changed saving of persons in specific birth cohorts are responsible for changes in the aggregate saving rate. Boskin and Lau embedded measures of the age distribution in a model of aggregate consumption and reported a significant difference in the propensity

17. The discrepancy is even larger if the dependent young are included. The child dependency rate dropped very sharply before 1980s, but it has been quite stable in recent decades. While of limited significance for the U.S. situation, demographic change will be discussed again in chapter 4 in the context of the international diversity of saving rates.

Figure 3-4. *Aged Dependency Rates in the Developed Economies, 1950–2020*[a]

Percent of population aged 15–64

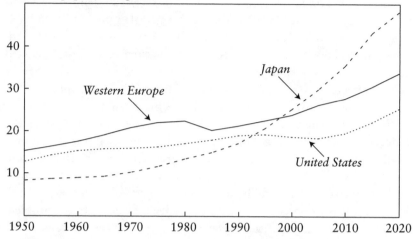

Source: United Nations (2011).
a. "Aged dependency" is defined as persons age 65 and over as a percentage of the population age 15 to 64 years.

to save between households born before and after 1939 (Boskin and Lau 1988). In contrast, Bosworth, Burtless, and Sabelhaus (1991) concludes from microsurvey data of the 1980s that the fall in saving rates was a general phenomenon that extended across age groups. Subsequent studies did find cohort differences but associated the reduced saving with different birth cohorts. Attanasio used data from the CEX for the years of 1980–91 to argue that the drop in aggregate saving was the result of lower saving by the cohort born during the years of 1920–39 (Attanasio 1998). Parker relied on similar microsurvey data to construct saving data for specific age cohorts for 1979–94; he concluded that the effect was more pervasive as successive birth cohorts were saving less than previous generations (Parker 2000).

Parker, as discussed above, relied on an adjustment to the microdata that has become less plausible in the years since his research was published. Given the size of the discrepancy between the average of the survey and the aggregate statistics shown in figure 3-2, it is not evident that the CEX provides meaningful measures of cohort differences. Furthermore, both Attanasio and Parker obtained their results by assuming the absence of any general sustained influence on saving over the period of analysis. While the microdata are potentially a very rich source of information on behavioral variations that can be related to differences in age, birth cohort, or individual year effects, not all three effects can be measured without imposing additional restrictions because they are linear combinations of one another: age = year (period) – year of birth (cohort). Both researchers chose an identifying constraint that the year effects averaged zero, forcing any sustained change in saving to be attributed to age or cohort effects. Given the large and continuing decline in saving in the years after their studies, that assumption seems debatable.

Finally, Gokhale, Kotlikoff, and Sabelhaus (1996) attributes the reduced saving to the large transfer of income and wealth from younger to older households through government transfers—Social Security pensions and Medicare. In addition, the authors point to a marked increase in the propensity of the elderly to spend the resources under their control. However, this explanation of the saving decline encounters a problem of timing, since the expansion of Social Security and the introduction of Medicare preceded the decline of the saving rate by several decades.

The magnitude of the fall in the aggregate saving rate, which continued to grow in the year after these studies were published, seems too large to attribute to the behavior of a few individual birth cohorts.

Wealth Effects

Wealth plays a primary role in the standard life-cycle model of household consumption behavior. The central hypothesis is that households should accumulate wealth during their working life in expectation of a decline in their earned income during retirement. Similarly, wealth can serve as a short-run buffer against unanticipated changes in their current income or unexpected expenditures. While wealth changes are the consequence of a large number of other consumer decisions, they also are subject to their own shocks due to changes in asset prices. If households experience an unexpected change in their wealth, they will revise their consumption plan. The life-cycle framework also suggests that the consumption response to a favorable wealth shock will be spread over the expected remaining life, so that the optimal increment to annual consumption is a function of the remaining life expectancy and the interest rate. In an example provided by Poterba (2000), a planning horizon of thirty years and a 3 percent real return would allow a household to raise consumption by 5 cents for each $1.00 increase in wealth.

The effect of wealth on consumption has taken special prominence in the discussion of the decline in saving in the 1990s because the reduction in saving coincided with a dramatic run-up in the wealth-income ratio, and the recent fall in wealth valuations has led to speculation that the saving rate might reverse its prior trend. Furthermore, the effect of wealth changes on consumption may depend on the source of the change. For example, increased equity prices might result from either higher expected future profits/dividends or a reduction in the rate by which future dividends are discounted. The former provide additional future resources and can be expected to raise spending, but the latter may not because the discounted value of planned future consumption would also have increased. The importance of equities has been dismissed because only 18 percent of households held such assets in the 2007 SCF. However, the percentage rises to 30 percent with the inclusion of investment funds. More relevant to the concern in the aggregate analysis with the average dollar rather than the average family, equities represent about a third of all wealth.

The influence of changes in home equity on consumption has been especially controversial. As mentioned in chapter 2, a few economists have argued that homeownership is simply a hedge against future rent increases and that to the extent that changes in home prices are correlated with expectations of future rent increases, there is no windfall gain to support increased consumption. Others have emphasized the historical role of credit constraints and down payment requirements to argue that home price increases would require potential first-time homebuyers to increase their saving, while existing homeowners had only a limited ability to borrow against their home equity. Thus, home price increases might actually reduce consumption. A third perspective emphasizes the liberalization of mortgage credit markets in recent decades and the improvement in their efficiency, which reduced down payment requirements and made it less costly to borrow against home equity; hence higher home values were more likely to translate into increased consumption.

There has been less controversy at the empirical level, where a large number of studies have found a marginal propensity to consume (MPC) out of wealth in the neighborhood of about 0.05. It suggests that when the wealth-income ratio rose from an average of 4.5 before 1985 to above 6 in the mid-2000s, it might have contributed to a reduction in the saving rate of 7 to 8 percentage points, an amount equal to the full magnitude of observed decline. An extensive survey of the issues and research through the 1990s is provided in Poterba (2000). In recent years, more of the research has focused on how the effects might differ across categories of wealth—primarily home equity versus financial wealth—and the interaction with changes in credit availability and mortgage refinancing.

Case, Quigley, and Shiller (2005) focused specifically on the relative effect of home equity and corporate stock. The authors examined the evidence for both U.S. states and a panel of other industrial countries and concluded that the evidence of a significant effect of home price variations on consumption was actually stronger than for corporate equities.[18] Slacalek used data from sixteen OECD countries to estimate the MPC out of wealth and disaggregated by housing and nonhousing wealth (Slacalek 2009). He found an average MPC of about 5 percent but considerable variation across the sample of countries, with the largest effect among the Anglo-Saxon countries. Slacalek attributed the variation to differences in the degree of financial market development. He found that the magnitude of the wealth effect was similar for housing and nonhousing wealth but that the former increased in recent times as it became easier to borrow against home equity. Using a different methodology, Carroll and others also found evidence of a strong housing wealth effect, but they emphasized the lags in which the impact on consumption built up from a low initial effect to about 9 percent after several years (Carroll, Otsuka, and Slacalek 2011). Aron and others report a significant long-run wealth effect of 0.04, but with a long lag (Aron and others 2010). They conclude that the marginal propensity to consume out of wealth is largest for liquid assets, followed by housing and corporate equity. They also emphasize strong interactions among changes in credit availability, increased mortgage liquidity, and the growth of housing.

Several studies have also examined the wealth effect by using survey data that make it possible to identify households that do and do not own the specific assets. Because only a minority of U.S. households actually hold corporate equities directly, some economists argued that their significance as a determinant of consumption at the aggregate level might reflect the correlation between the stock market and consumer confidence (Romer 1990). The household-level data conceptually make it possible to identify

---

18. There is agreement that the short-run effects on consumption of equity price changes are damped because of the considerable size of the transitory variations.

equity holders and distinguish between the two channels. However, because of the extreme concentration of wealth, the available surveys, with their relatively small size, are unlikely to be fully representative of holders of large amounts of wealth. That under-representation of those wealth holders was shown to be a problem for the PSID in figure 3-3.

Parker (2000) did report a large effect of wealth changes on consumption using data from the PSID. The PSID does not actually ask households about consumption, however, and the conclusions were based on an imputation of the ratio of total consumption to food purchases from the CEX. Several other studies have used the PSID data to infer responses to changes in wealth. They use information on the change in wealth holdings to estimate the change in active saving directly. Engelhardt (1996a), which focused on the change between the 1984 and 1989 waves of the PSID, reported a significant negative effect of housing valuation changes on saving but no impact of capital gains outside of housing. Juster and others (2006), which extended the analysis to include the 1994 wave of the PSID, reported a small effect of housing but a very large impact from changes in corporate equities. In this study, I did attempt to extend the analysis of the Engelhardt and Juster and others studies to later waves of the PSID. However, the effort failed to demonstrate a consistent correlation between wealth and saving.

Credit Conditions

The financial opportunities faced by American household have changed in major ways over the past several decades (Dynan 2009). Significant changes in the mortgage market expanded access to homeownership—for example, by requiring little or no down payment—and many homeowners used the ease of refinancing to withdraw home equity. The result was a fundamental change in the response to higher home prices: while there was still a small negative effect on the spending of potential first-time homebuyers, there was a larger positive effect on the spending of existing homeowners who were able to borrow against their increased home equity. Technological innovations made it easier for lenders to assess the creditworthiness of prospective borrowers, and they developed new approaches to managing risk. The ease of refinancing also reduced the need for precautionary saving balances. Individuals who used to save in anticipation of major purchases were increasingly able to make a purchase by borrowing and do their saving afterward, through repayment of the debt.

The link between financial innovations and consumer behavior is most evident in mortgage markets: the mortgage became a much more liquid financial instrument that could be used to extract home equity. Greenspan and Kennedy (2008) developed measures of the total volume of mortgage refinancing and home-equity extraction. Their estimate of mortgage refinancing, whereby an existing loan is replaced with a new loan on the same property, is shown in panel A of figure 3-5. Refinancing ranged between $0.2 trillion and $1 trillion in the 1990s, when interest rates fluctuated in the 7 to 8 percent range, down from the 10 percent levels of the late 1980s, but activity exploded in 2002–04, when mortgage interest rates dropped below 6 percent, reaching a peak of $3 trillion in 2003.

If the old loan is replaced with one of the same size, there would be little consequence for saving, but it became increasingly common to increase the face amount of the loan to extract some of the accumulated equity. Panel B of figure 3-5 reports the extraction of home equity both through home equity loans and increases in the size of the mortgage at the time of refinancing. Both forms of equity withdrawal increased over the past two decades, but home equity loans show a more consistent pattern of growth, right up to the bursting of the housing bubble in 2007. They rose from less than 1 percent of household disposable income in the early and mid-1990s to more than 5 percent in 2004–06. Both forms of withdrawal have nearly stopped since the financial crisis. However, information on the use of equity extractions is limited because of incomplete information. A portion of the funds was reinvested in home improvements, and some may have been allocated to financial investments and debt consolidation. The portion devoted to consumption is uncertain.

The increase in the ability to borrow has been found to be associated with the reduction in saving. In a 2007 study, Muellbauer created an index of credit availability based on a Federal Reserve survey question on banks' willingness to make loans for the purchase of consumer durables (Muellbauer 2007). He demonstrated a significant correlation between saving and credit availability. Subsequently, in the 2010 *Economic Report of the President,* the Council of Economic Advisers developed a simple statistical model that relates the saving rate to the wealth-income ratio, a version of the measure of the credit availability used by Muellbauer, and the unemployment rate in order to illustrate the contribution of these factors to the reduction in saving. The council's statistical model is re-estimated for the period of 1966 through 2010, with the following results:

Figure 3-5. *Mortgage Market Activity, 1991–2008*

Panel A. Mortgage refinancings

Billions of 2000 dollars

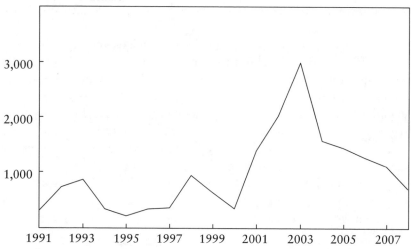

Panel B. Home equity extraction

Billions of 2000 dollars

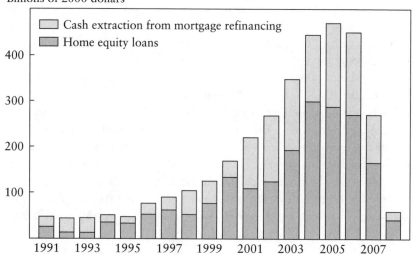

Source: Kennedy and Greenspan (2008).

a. Data exclude equity extracted through home sales; dollar values are converted to constant prices of 2000.

(1) $S/Y = -1.5 \times (W/Y)_{-1} - 0.4 \times CRED + 0.25 \times UR + 15.6,$
              (4.8)   (11.1)   (3.0)   (8.9)

where S/Y = household saving rate (percentage); $(W/Y)_{-1}$ = household wealth-income ratio, beginning of period; $CRED$ = credit availability index; and UR = unemployment rate (percentage).[19]

All three terms are statistically significant and have the expected signs. The coefficient on the wealth-income ratio is somewhat smaller than has been typical in the research that was discussed earlier, but an effort to increase the long-run response by the addition of lags was ineffective. Figure 3-6 shows the actual saving rate and the predicted rate from the regression. The regression performs very well in capturing the long-term deterioration in the saving rate and some of the major cyclical movements. It does especially well in accounting for the large turnaround in the saving rate during the financial crisis. It does less well in tracking the short-run changes in the quarterly data, but those errors may reflect a considerable amount of statistical noise.

Ricardian Equivalence

The Ricardian equivalence paradigm argues that variations in government budget balances will be fully offset by adjustments in private saving (Barro 1974). Rational taxpayers will understand that all government spending must be paid for sooner or later; therefore they will adjust their own saving in anticipation of required changes in future taxes. The derivation of the offset requires several restrictive assumptions. In particular, it is assumed that taxpayers are not subject to liquidity constraints and can borrow freely, and the consumption behavior of successive generations is linked through pooling of their resources. While the requirements for full Ricardian equivalence seem unlikely to be met in reality, a substantial number of empirical studies have found a significant private sector offset to changes in public saving. There are good reasons for thinking that the correlation would not be negligible. In the short run, private saving would be expected to decline in response to an increase in taxes simply because the marginal propensity to spend out of disposable income is not unity.

---

19. $R^2 = 0.91$; SE = 0.8; T statistics in parentheses, Newey-West estimates. The credit index is computed quarterly as the proportion of banks indicating increased willingness to make consumer installment loans multiplied by the ratio of consumer debt to disposable income. The result is then cumulated beginning in 1966.

Figure 3-6. *Actual and Predicted Saving Rate, 1965–2010*

Percent of disposable income

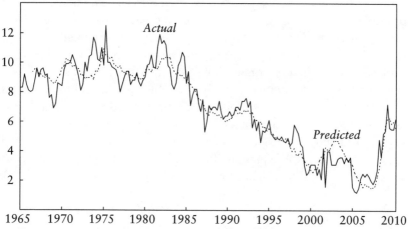

Sources: Bureau of Economic Analysis (2011a); Board of Governors of the Federal Reserve (2011a); and author's calculations from equation 1 in text.

Furthermore, the public and private sector share common endogenous responses to cyclical fluctuations in the overall economy. Even in the longer term, increased public sector borrowing within a closed economy near full employment could raise interest rates and crowd out private spending.

Since Barro raised the issue, a large literature has explored the topic, theoretically and empirically.[20] The issue emerged again in the aftermath of the 2008–09 financial crisis as part of the debate over the efficacy of the fiscal stimulus measures. Unfortunately, all that research has not led to a consensus on the magnitude of the offset. Many of the recent empirical studies have relied on international panel data sets because they yield a larger range of experience. Using data for the OECD countries up through 2008, Röhn concluded that the offset was about 40 percent, but with considerable cross-country heterogeneity: the estimated offset was largest for changes in revenues and smallest for public investment (Röhn 2010). He also found support for the argument of Perotti (1999) that nonlinearities would increase the response of private saving for countries with high existing debt levels because citizens are more likely to regard the current situation as unsustainable.

20. A useful recent survey is Ricciuti (2003).

Recent studies of saving in the United States have not emphasized the offset to public sector deficits as a primary explanation for the fall in private saving. In the face of a large swing in the government budget over the past two decades, from deficit to surplus and back to deficit, the private saving rate continued its secular decline. The alternative explanation—the rise in the wealth-income ratio—appears as a simpler and more plausible explanation for the fall in household saving. A similar issue arises with respect to the 2008–09 financial crisis, in which public and private rates of saving displayed strong inverse movements, yet the huge wealth loss again emerges as a more direct explanation for the rise in household saving. As a simple test, government saving and net government lending were both included in equation 1 above, but the coefficients were both small and statistically insignificant.

Corporate Veil

In the national accounts, corporate saving (retained earnings) is shown as a component of national saving separate from the saving of households. Yet from an economic perspective the line between the two is somewhat arbitrary. In the U.S. accounts, sole proprietorships and partnerships are classified with households. Yet S corporations, a small-firm classification with favorable tax treatment, are included within the corporate sector. They have grown over the past decade to represent about 25 percent of corporate profits, but all earnings must be fully passed through as dividends to their shareholders.

The argument that individual stockholders will pierce the "corporate veil" and treat the saving of the corporation as equivalent to their own rests on the same principles as those of "Ricardian equivalence," but the assertion seems stronger because it does not require an assumption of altruistic intergenerational linkages; the corporation's value is readily determined in the market. The issue has taken on somewhat greater importance in recent years because of the growing importance of corporate saving in many countries (OECD 2007). It also arises in discussions of shifts in the relative tax burden between corporations and individuals (Poterba 1987) and of whether those shifts alter household saving.

The standard neoclassical model suggests that absent tax effects, the consumption decisions of stockholders should be unaffected by changes in the distribution of corporate income between dividends and retained earnings. Consumption is formulated as a function of the present value of current and future labor earning plus the current value of financial assets, and in a friction-free world, the latter term would be unchanged by variations in the structure of capital income receipts. However, financial transactions do have tax implications and are subject to various transaction costs, and behavioral models often perceive a distinction between current income and changes in asset valuations. It is also common, therefore, to relate household consumption to current disposable income and household wealth. Since the marginal propensity to spend out of income is usually an order of magnitude greater than the marginal propensity to spend out of wealth, it would appear that shifting corporate income from retained earnings, which would reduce stock market value, to dividends would increase consumption by the difference between the two propensities.

In practice, it has been as difficult to resolve the question of whether consumers pierce the corporate veil as it is to determine the role of Ricardian equivalence. Again, both corporate saving and household saving are highly endogenous and subject to many common influences. Therefore, most of the research has sought to find independent exogenous changes in corporate dividend policy that could be used to identify the degree of integration of corporate and household saving. Using aggregate data, Poterba (1987) concludes that changes in corporate saving are not completely offset by compensating adjustments of household saving and that a $1 increase in corporate saving would raise private saving by 25 cents to 50 cents. Baker and others, using microsurvey data, reached a similar conclusion, of a less-than-full offset (Baker, Nagel, and Wurgler 2007). Still, the offsets are sufficient to suggest that it is important to evaluate changes in corporate and household saving in a joint fashion. Changes in U.S. tax policy over the past three decades, however, have reduced the benefits of sheltering income within corporations, and that would appear to argue against a shift of saving from households to corporations as an explanation for the fall in household saving.

Conclusion

This chapter reviews the various explanations for the fall in household saving from the perspective of data on the aggregate economy and surveys of individual households. In line with the life-cycle model of saving, aggregate household saving from the flow of funds accounts has been separated between saving in formal retirement plans and more discretionary forms of saving. A portion of the fall in the saving rate can be traced to lower rates of asset accumulation within private pension plans. Saving within pension plans has slowed as the programs have become more mature and benefits have risen relative to new contributions. This is especially evident in private defined benefit plans, whose financial difficulties and aging contributor base have been widely publicized. There also has been a substantial reduction of saving within public pension programs and the newer defined contribution plans, but the slowing of the defined contribution plans is offset by the large transfer of funds into IRAs. We might look forward to a modest recovery of pension saving in the short run as recent losses in the equity markets will require larger employer contributions. Nonetheless, it seems evident that pension saving will remain below past peaks because the existing plans are reaching maturity and the pension system is not expanding to cover a larger portion of the workforce. However, the largest reduction in saving has been outside of formal retirement accounts. The drop in this component occurred largely during the 1980s, fluctuated around zero in the 1990s, and turned sharply negative in the 2000s. It is also the component that surged in the aftermath of the financial crisis.

Analysis of the principal causes of the reduced saving emphasizes the role of large wealth gains during the 1990s and 2000s and the easing of credit restrictions, principally in the residential mortgage market. The chapter also argues that despite its emphasis within the life-cycle model, demographic change does not appear to be a significant factor, nor can the reduced saving be attributed to a specific age cohort of households. Finally, there is only a very loose correlation between changes in public and private sector saving.

The study has been less successful in its effort to use microsurvey data to explore further the potential causes of reduced rates of saving and in particular to determine whether the fall in the saving rate was a general phenomenon or restricted to a few socioeconomic groups. It appears that the surveys are not able to obtain meaningful responses when individuals are asked to distinguish between increments to their wealth that result from active saving decisions and those that result from changes in asset prices. Therefore, while the surveys do confirm the wealth accumulation shown in the aggregate data, they do not trace a pattern of declining saving. The wealth data, however, do not support the hypothesis of a concentration of reduced saving among a few socioeconomic groups; the wealth gains are evident for all groups and are largest among older households and those with high levels of education.

CHAPTER FOUR

Global Saving Patterns

Concerns about the balance of saving and investment at the global level have motivated research on saving for several decades. In the 1990s, studies of the impact of population aging on public budget balances and private sector saving generated worries about a looming scarcity of saving in the global economy, with its attendant pressures for rising real interest rates.[1] Institutions such as the International Monetary Fund (IMF) and the Organization for Economic Cooperation and Development (OECD) issued reports on what they perceived to be a potential crisis. However, in the first decades of the 2000s, the attention of government policymakers turned 180 degrees to the notion of a glut of global saving (Bernanke 2005). Such a shift of emphasis was especially unexpected from the perspective of the United States, where the public discussion had focused on an ongoing decline of private saving and the reemergence of large budget deficits. Certainly, the United States has not been plagued by an oversupply of saving. The absence of saving in the United States, in conjunction with strong domestic investment opportunities, has created a current account deficit of unprecedented size, peaking at $800 billion in 2006.

However, while one can be astounded by the size of the U.S. deficits, the ease with which they have been financed at the global level is equally surprising. Therefore, there are two perspectives on the global saving imbalance: why is there a large saving shortfall in the United States, and why is there such a large excess of saving in the rest of the world? Furthermore, given that this has all occurred against the backdrop of low real interest rates around the globe, it can be asserted, as Bernanke did,

---

1. See, for example, OECD (1996), McKinsey Global Institute (1994), and IMF (1995).

that the greater puzzle is the excess saving in the rest of the world. Many researchers attribute the saving surplus in part to demographic change or, more specifically, to the anticipation of future population aging and its attendant retirement costs in the other industrial countries. In that view, high saving today results from the early phase of a demographic change that will impose a cycle of surplus followed by a substantial reduction in saving at the global level. However, Bernanke focused his remarks on an unexpected reversal of capital flows to emerging markets. In the aftermath of the Asian financial crisis, several of those economies became large net lenders.

This chapter is devoted to an examination of recent changes in the balance of saving and investment from a global perspective. While others have emphasized the role of demographic change in first promoting and then depressing rates of national saving in industrial countries, this analysis argues that the more pervasive changes have been in declining rates of investment in both industrial and developing countries. The discussion also highlights the wide diversity of saving trends across countries. That variation provides an opportunity to explore some of the most popular reasons given for variation in saving rates and to observe their applicability in different national contexts.

This chapter first provides a global overview of recent trends in saving and investment that addresses some of the above concerns. It is based on aggregate measures of national saving and investment for about eighty-five countries over the period of 1980–2008. It then provides more detailed discussion of saving trends in other advanced economies (such as Canada, Japan, and Europe) that offers contrasts with and some insights into the U.S. experience. It concludes with an examination of saving behavior in China and India.

Global Imbalances

National patterns of saving and investment are linked globally through a simple accounting identity in which the difference between national saving and investment is equal to the external balance with the rest of the world, the current account:

$$(1) \qquad\qquad CA = S - I.$$

Furthermore, absent errors and omissions, the sum of the current accounts across all economies should equal zero. Thus, the deficits of some countries will be offset by the surpluses of others. Prior to the 1970s, current account imbalances were strictly limited, as most national financial markets operated as closed systems.[2] With the emergence of large-scale cross-border capital flows, countries have become capable of financing increasingly large imbalances on a sustained basis.

The dichotomy in the world economy between the external position of the United States and everyone else is highlighted in table 4-1, which shows the current account balances for major regions in the world economy over the period of 1980–2010, providing a simple summary of the magnitude and distribution of the saving-investment (S-I) imbalances. The United States clearly stands out for the size of its recent deficit, which is matched by surpluses in all other regions. At the same time, Europe's surplus has grown modestly since the mid-1990s, and Japan's surplus has remained basically unchanged for nearly a quarter of a century. Similarly, little has changed in Latin America. The offsets to the increased U.S. deficit are large surpluses in the emerging economies of Asia and the oil-producing economies of the Middle East.[3] Given the rise of oil prices, the surge of saving within the oil-producing regions is not a surprise, but the sudden emergence of a large excess of saving over investment in Asia is less expected. There is also a substantial current account discrepancy

2. Feldstein and Horioka (1980) noted the extremely high correlation between national rates of saving and investment and interpreted it as implying a very limited mobility of capital across national borders. While that empirical finding remains robust, the magnitude of the correlation has declined over the years, consistent with the development of increasingly integrated global markets. Subsequent research has also shown that the Feldstein-Horioka correlation may not be a reliable indicator of capital mobility: a wide variety of domestic shocks can induce national saving and domestic investment to change in a coordinated fashion independent of any constraints on the flow of capital and goods across a nation's borders. In addition, cross-border substitutability in goods and services trade, despite increases in recent decades, still tends to be relatively low; in any event, it is markedly less than cross-border financial substitutability. Accordingly, the high correlation between domestic investment and national saving may be attributable much more to rigidities in goods markets than to a lack of integration among financial markets. Frankel (1992) and Obstfeld and Rogoff (1996) review the alternative interpretations of the Feldstein-Horioka findings and their implications for global capital flows.

3. "Emerging Asia" is a broad category that includes the newly industrialized economies (Hong Kong, Singapore, South Korea, and Taiwan) as well as developing economies such as China and India. Complete definitions are provided in table 4-1. The residual category of other countries is largely composed of Africa, Eastern Europe, and South Asia (excluding India).

Table 4-1. *Current Account as Percent of World GDP, Selected Regions and Years*

Region	1980–89	1990–99	2000–05	2006–08	2009	2010
United States	−0.50	−0.43	−1.41	−1.37	−0.72	−0.79
Japan	0.26	0.36	0.35	0.33	0.24	0.24
Europe[a]	−0.01	0.08	0.23	0.16	0.11	0.18
Emerging Asia[b]	−0.01	0.06	0.38	0.87	0.81	0.78
Emerging Latin America[c]	−0.11	−0.14	−0.02	0.04	−0.02	−0.06
Middle East[d]	0.13	−0.04	0.21	0.49	0.10	0.23
Other countries	−0.31	−0.21	0.00	−0.11	−0.21	−0.18
Discrepancy	0.54	0.30	0.27	−0.41	−0.32	−0.41

Source: International Monetary Fund (2011a).

a. Austria, Belgium, Denmark, Finland, France, Germany, Greece, Ireland, Italy, Netherlands, Norway, Portugal, Spain, Sweden, Switzerland, and the United Kingdom.

b. China, Hong Kong, India, Indonesia, Malaysia, Philippines, Singapore, South Korea, Taiwan, and Thailand. First column average is for 1982–89.

c. Argentina, Brazil, Chile, Colombia, Ecuador, Mexico, Peru, and Venezuela.

d. Bahrain, Egypt, Iran, Jordan, Kuwait, Lebanon, Libya, Oman, Qatar, Saudi Arabia, Syria, United Arab Emirates, and Yemen.

at the global level.[4] Historically, the discrepancy was thought to arise primarily because of the under-reporting of investment income and transportation services, but in the last decade it has changed sign as countries are reporting more receipts than payments, largely in the area of business services (IMF 2009, p. 35).

We can get a clearer picture of the evolving balances by focusing separately on the changes in rates of national saving and investment. Unlike in the previous chapters, here both saving and investment are reported gross of capital consumption allowances since many countries do not provide estimates of capital depreciation. The U.S. balance, shown in panel A of figure 4-1, is dominated by an ongoing decline in the saving rate that began in the early 1980s. As discussed in chapter 2, household saving has steadily fallen over the period, and after a major improvement in the 1990s, the public sector budget balance fell back into substantial deficit in the first decade of the 2000s. Only corporate saving has held

---

4. The IMF reports the discrepancy as the sum of the current accounts across all reporting countries. In table 4-1, the sign is reversed so that the current accounts will sum to zero.

Figure 4-1. *Saving and Investment, Regional Averages, 1980–2009*
Percent of gross national income

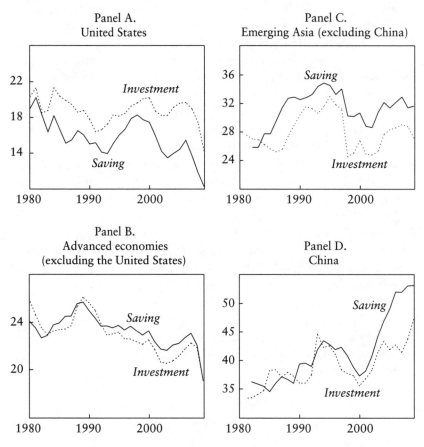

Sources: World Bank (2011); Organization for Economic Cooperation and Development (2011); International Monetary Fund (2011b).

up in recent years, as profits soared after the 2001 recession. Since the financial crisis, a recovery of household saving has been more than offset by very large fiscal deficits. On the other side of the balance, the United States continued to offer very good investment opportunities, superior to those of most other industrial countries up until the crisis. Therefore, the investment rate showed no secular pattern of deterioration comparable to that for saving. The combination of good investment opportunities and very little domestic saving with which to finance them has translated into an ever-growing reliance on the net inflow of resources from abroad. While the degree of reliance on foreign financing is unprecedented, it was achieved with relatively little strain because foreigners also perceived the United States as offering very attractive investment opportunities. The primary cost is that the strong demand for dollar-denominated assets kept the value of the dollar at a high level and greatly weakened the ability of U.S. firms to compete in global markets.

Bernanke argued that the low U.S. saving has been offset by an increase in global saving, including that of other industrial countries, and he emphasized demographic change as a major source of the increase, arguing that saving should be rising in anticipation of retirement. However, as shown in panel B of figure 4-1, rates of both saving and investment have steadily fallen in other industrial countries. In fact, the greater contrast with the experience of the United States is actually on the investment side. Rates of investment deteriorated in both Japan and Europe since 1990, contrasting with the stability of the U.S. rate. This is undoubtedly due to their weak growth in recent decades. With parallel reductions in rates of saving and investment, Europe and Japan averaged small external surpluses.

Some of the fall in saving within the other industrial countries can be attributed to deterioration in the public sector balance that was even more pronounced than in the United States. Many of these countries formerly used strong public saving to supplement the private sector and to support efforts to catch up to U.S. living standards. When they encountered economic problems in the 1980s (Europe) and 1990s (Japan), the surpluses disappeared. The result is that the rates of national saving and investment in other industrial countries have gradually fallen toward those of the United States.

The most striking increase in the S-I balance is in emerging Asia, where countries have long been notable for high and rising rates of saving.[5] It also appears that those high saving rates were concentrated in the private sector, since the governments generally avoided large budget surpluses or deficits. Several explanations have been put forth for this pattern of saving behavior. First, the sharp decline in birth rates has lowered the child dependency rate (ratio of persons age 0–14 to those age 15–64 years) and encouraged adults to save for retirement since they can no longer

---

5. Our regional averages are constructed using commercial exchange rates to convert all of the data into a common currency.

simply rely on their children; moreover, many of these countries have underdeveloped public retirement systems. Second, high growth creates a virtuous circle in which rapid income growth makes it easy to save at the same time that one's standard of living is improving, and the high saving feeds back through capital accumulation to promote further growth. This explanation received additional support when saving rates actually fell for a time after the Asian financial crisis, when growth slowed.[6] Third, it is argued that some Asian countries have traditions of strong intergenerational ties that may serve to promote dynastic saving and a longer-term perspective on wealth accumulation.

It is increasingly important, however, to distinguish between China and the rest of emerging Asia. In recent years, China's saving rate has diverged from that of other countries in East Asia, and its rapid growth makes it an increasingly dominant influence on the regional average (panels C and D in figure 4-1). Most important, the shift in the S-I balance within the Asian economies other than China can be traced primarily to changes on the investment side. The 1997 financial crisis had its greatest impact on investment spending, which fell precipitously; although the affected economies have recovered to a large extent, the rate of investment has not been restored to pre-crisis levels, even after nearly ten years. The evidence of a surge of saving is concentrated in China, where the saving rate has risen sharply from already high levels. In contrast, the investment rate leveled out in the years after China's accession to the World Trade Organization (WTO), opening up a large gap between saving and investment that translated into a very large external deficit until the financial crisis in 2009. In the crisis, global trade shrank at an unprecedented rate, and in response, China enacted a very large domestic stimulus that offset much of the loss of exports.

Some issues also arise for India as it grows in economic importance. It has seen large increases in both saving and investment, but the two have remained in relatively close balance. If India were removed from panel C of figure 4-1, the drop-off in rates of investment would be even more pronounced. The saving-investment balance of India is addressed more specifically later in the chapter.

6. The emphasis on a positive correlation with income change, however, is contrary to the perspective of the life-cycle model, under which expectations of strong future income growth should reduce current saving (Tobin 1967).

Still, the combination of lower rates of investment outside China and increased Chinese saving resulted in a large net external surplus in the first decade of the 2000s for the region as a whole. It is also remarkable that much of the surplus emerged in the form of increased official holdings of foreign exchange reserves. In the aftermath of the 1997–98 Asian financial crisis, many countries concluded that they could not rely on the international agencies to respond in a timely fashion and that they needed to self-insure against future crises by accumulating larger reserves. Others have seen reserve accumulation as a means of holding down their exchange rate and improving their competitiveness. In both instances, the surplus of the domestic S-I balance has spilled into international markets.

Overall, the surprise at the global level is that the story appears to be one of weak investment rather than a rise in saving. Also, this initial examination does not seem to support the emphasis on demographic change in other industrial countries as a significant factor in recent developments, given their general declining pattern of saving. The most striking aspect, however, is the diversity of trends in both rates of saving and investment across the global economy; those differences in the international experience are potentially an important means of better understanding the saving behavior at the national level. This aspect is explored in a discussion of several countries that follows below.

Finally, we can also observe a secular decline in global interest rates (figure 4-2) that also suggests a growing surplus of saving over investment. However, the long-term nature of the fall in real interest rates, extending back to the early 1990s, does not reflect a sudden emergence of a saving glut. The figure uses two measures of the real interest rates to highlight that aspect. The first is the U.S. government ten-year bond rate adjusted for expected price inflation. The second is an average of real interest rates in the four major financial centers: the United States, the United Kingdom, Germany, and Japan. National interest rates have converged as financial markets became more integrated, and the two measures show remarkably similar patterns of fluctuation within a declining secular trend.

Major Countries

A significant number of countries, mainly advanced economies of the OECD, compile information on saving and investment by major sector, such as government, corporations, and households. Those measures are shown and discussed here for Canada, Japan, and an average of the major

Figure 4-2. *Global Interest Rates, 1980–2010*[a]

Percent

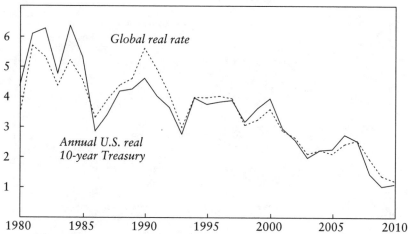

Sources: Organization for Economic Cooperation and Development (2011); Federal Reserve Bank of Philadelphia (2011).

a. The global rate is calculated as the average of real interest rates in the four major financial centers: the United States, the United Kingdom, Germany, and Japan. The country weights are 0.5, 0.25, 0.125, and 0.125, respectively. Expected inflation is measured as a centered ten-year average of the change in the consumer price index. The U.S. real rate uses the Treasury ten-year bond rate and a forecast of inflation from the Federal Reserve Bank of Philadelphia.

European economies. These countries afford the most relevant comparisons with the United States, and they serve to highlight the diversity in patterns of national saving. In addition, detailed estimates for China and India are discussed because they provide interesting illustrations of saving behavior under conditions of very rapid economic growth.

Canada

Canadian saving behavior provides an interesting and puzzling comparison with that of the United States. The household saving rate in Canada, which had moved in tandem with the U.S. saving rate throughout the 1950s and 1960s, rose sharply in the early 1970s and reached an average of 17 percent of disposable income in the first half of the 1980s (panel A of figure 4-3); the U.S. rate, in contrast, was 10 percent. The increase attracted considerable attention from economists interested in

Figure 4-3. *Canada Saving, Wealth, and Consumption, 1970–2010*

Panel A. Household saving

Percent of national disposable income

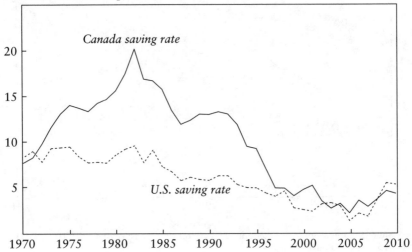

Panel B. Consumption, wealth, and capital gain

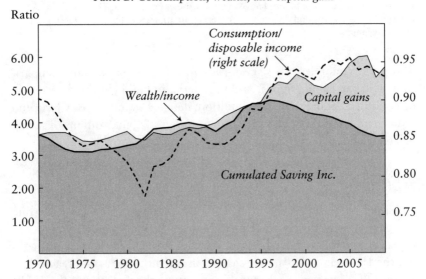

Sources: Statistics Canada (2011a, table 3); Statistics Canada (2011b, table 5); and author's calculations.

saving behavior, and several studies sought to relate the higher saving to the expansion of Canadian tax incentives for retirement saving in the early 1970s.[7] But then, with equal abruptness, the Canadian saving rate began to fall and continued to do so throughout the 1990s; by the middle of the first decade of the 2000s, it had returned to a level comparable to that of the United States.

This divergence in saving rates is especially interesting because many aspects of economic performance within the two countries, including inflation, interest rates, and unemployment, remained linked through trade and capital movements across a very open border. Plus, the countries would seem to share many common social characteristics and institutions.[8] Furthermore, in most countries, including the United States, the household saving rate has changed only gradually over extended periods, and given the potential for measurement errors in national accounts, it has been difficult to reach strong conclusions about the major determinants of saving on the basis of past changes. In this regard, the magnitude of change in the Canadian rate is among the largest for major industrial countries, and the opportunity that it offers to explore saving behavior is enhanced by the availability of surveys of individual household saving that extend over the full period of the rise and fall in the saving rate.

Canada has also experienced wide variations in other components of national saving (table 4-2). Government saving was highly negative between 1975 and 1995, and that was one reason, in addition to tax advantages, that Carroll and Summers (1987) advanced Ricardian equivalence as an explanation for the initial rise in household saving in the late 1970s.[9] After 1995, the government reversed course and generated substantial budget surpluses that went a long distance toward paying off the public debt prior to the 2008–09 financial crisis. In addition, Canada experienced a large rise in the corporate saving rate from an average of near 0 percent of national income in the early 1990s to 7 percent in the first decades of the 2000s. The result has been a large shift in the

7. See, in particular, Carroll and Summers (1987), Jump and Wilson (1986), and Beach, Boadway, and Bruce (1988). Canada also differs from the United States in that it does not provide an income tax deduction for mortgage interest payments.

8. For example, the United States has a slightly higher mean income, but median incomes are higher in Canada because it has fewer very poor and very rich families. For a recent comparison of the income distribution of Canada and the United States, see Saez and Veall (2005).

9. See the discussion of Ricardian equivalence in chapter 3.

Table 4-2. *Canadian Net Saving and Investment, 1980–2010*
Percent of net disposable income

Item	1970–79	1980–89	1990–99	2000–05	2006–10
Saving	6.1	9.9	5.3	11.2	9.7
Government	–0.6	–5.1	–4.2	1.9	–0.1
Private	13.3	15.0	9.5	9.3	9.8
Corporate	3.8	3.3	2.7	6.9	7.1
Household	9.5	11.6	6.8	2.4	2.7
Investment	14.5	11.7	7.6	8.5	10.8
Government	1.6	0.9	0.6	0.8	1.6
Private	12.9	10.8	7.0	7.7	9.2
Corporate	8.3	6.6	3.7	3.7	4.2
Household	4.6	4.2	3.3	4.0	5.0
Net capital transfers	0.3	0.6	1.1	0.5	0.3
Net lending	–1.6	–1.3	–1.2	3.2	–0.8

Source: Statistics Canada (2011b, table 15).

composition of national saving away from households to corporations and government.

MACROECONOMIC ANALYSIS. Two studies of the initial rise of Canadian household saving rates in the 1970s, Carroll and Summers (1987) and Jump and Wilson (1986), both emphasized the tax advantages of the Registered Retirement Saving Plan (RRSP) program, which preceded the introduction of individual retirement accounts in the United States.[10] However, it now seems evident that the accumulation of funds in the RRSPs was never large enough to account for the rise in saving during the 1970s, and they continued to grow in the years when the saving rate fell back below its historical average (Burbidge, Fretz, and Veall 1998).[11]

10. Jump and Wilson also adjusted Canadian saving for inflation, but while the adjustment had large offsetting impacts on the levels of government and household saving rates, it left the time patterns largely unchanged. They were also more doubtful that tax incentives could account for the difference between Canadian and U.S. household saving rates.

11. Additional details on the effects of RRSPs are discussed in Engelhardt (1996b) and Millwood (2002).

More recently, Bérubé and Côté (2000) emphasized the roles of the real rate of interest, expected inflation, the wealth-income ratio, and shifts in the government fiscal balance (Ricardian equivalence) as the primary explanations for the variation in household saving over the 1965–98 period. The authors attributed the sharp rise in the saving rate during the 1970s to a strong relationship with expected inflation and the emergence of a large and persistent government fiscal deficit. They perceived a fall in expected inflation as the primary factor in the reversal of the saving rate in the late 1980s, but they noted that a reduction in the fiscal deficit and a rise in the wealth-income ratio were also significant contributors to the continued low rate of saving in the 1990s and presumably into the 2000s.[12] The Bérubé and Côté estimates of the fiscal offset range between 0.5 and 0.8—a little higher than estimates for the United States—and the coefficient on the wealth-income ratio is between 2 and 4 percent. The potential influence of the wealth effect is highlighted in panel B of figure 4-3 by distinguishing between the role of accumulated saving and capital gains/losses (as is done with the United States in chapter 2) and comparing the rise in the wealth-income ratio with the variation in the share of household disposable income devoted to consumption. In many respects, the change in the Canadian wealth-income ratio since the mid-1990s and the increased role of capital gains corresponds with the experience in the United States. And the two countries have seen similar secular reductions in household saving rates. The very high saving rate of the early 1980s appears to reflect a greater sensitivity to mortgage interest rates. Because Canadians cannot obtain fixed-rate financing beyond five years, they faced a much greater exposure to the surge of interest rates in the early 1980s, and they responded with intense efforts to pay down their mortgage balances.

Another striking aspect of the Canadian saving experience is the fact that the decline in the household rate over the past two decades has been more than offset by increased saving within the corporate sector and the elimination of the prior government budget deficits. The rise in corporate saving is driven in turn by a substantial increase in the corporate profit rate. The Canadian national accounts do not identify dividends and interest payments separately, but in combination they have remained quite

12. Pichette and Tremblay (2003) focused on the role of wealth and found a significant negative influence of variations in housing wealth but not of equity values. They did not address the other aspects of the Bérubé and Côté study.

stable, so that the rise in profits translated into higher retained earnings–corporate saving. The result has been a surprisingly stable private saving rate throughout the last half of the 1990s and into the 2000s. In addition, a major fiscal consolidation in the mid-1990s resulted in a large increase in government saving that was maintained up to the 2008–09 financial crisis. The rise in corporate saving is also evident in the United States, but on a much smaller scale, and the fiscal improvement of the late 1990s was not sustained.

SURVEY DATA. Surveys offer the major advantage of providing additional information on the saving patterns of households with differing socioeconomic characteristics. Thus, when we observe the sharp rise in the aggregate saving rate in the years up to the early 1980s and its subsequent decline, it should be possible to observe the types of households whose saving behavior was responsible for the change. Unfortunately, as discussed in chapter 3, the successive household surveys in the United States fail to track the time pattern of change in the macroeconomic data. I attributed the discrepancy to measurement errors in the U.S. surveys and the problems that households encounter in accurately recalling prior expenditures.

However, the Canadian Survey of Household Spending (SHS) differs in some important respects from the comparable Consumer Expenditure Survey (CEX) in the United States. The survey is based on a larger sample of about 20,000 households—only 7,500 households are included in the CEX—and households are interviewed only once about income and expenditures in the prior year. Both surveys ask questions about financial transactions that make it possible to calculate saving as the change in net assets as well as income minus consumption. The U.S. data on financial assets and liabilities are of low quality due to respondents' resistance to providing information on the level of their wealth holdings, whereas the SHS asks about changes in financial assets and liabilities. Most important, the SHS incorporates the financial information in a "balanced edit" that computes a residual of receipts minus expenditures and the change in net assets as a check on the quality of the interview. For large discrepancies, the interviewer will go back to the household to resolve it or the record will not be used.[13]

13. The emphasis on the balance of receipts and disbursements seems to have improved the consistency of the saving estimates from the survey, but we do not know the frequency with which the balance edit triggered a revision of responses and whether it may have simply imposed an artificial constraint on respondents' answers.

Figure 4-4. *Canadian Household Saving Rate, According to National Accounts and the Survey of Household Spending*

Percent of disposable income

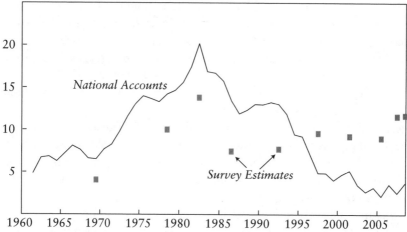

Sources: Statistics Canada (2011b, table 5); Statistics Canada (2011c); and author's calculations.

In the 1980s, Canada's household expenditure survey was one of the few among the OECD countries that corresponded with the time pattern of change in household saving as reported in the national accounts. Unfortunately, that has been less true over the past decade. The results of the survey from a selected set of years back to 1969 are shown in figure 4-4. The mean saving from the survey seems to reflect large portions of the rise in the saving rate from 1969 to the early 1980s and its decline throughout the 1980s. However, the survey reports a slight increase in the mean saving rate between 1992 and 2008, while the national accounts measure continues to fall.[14] Average saving rates are computed for various

14. As with the United States, there are important differences in the concepts used in the SHS and the national accounts. They include the exclusion from the survey of employer contributions to retirement accounts and the value of health services provided by the national health insurance program. Also, housing is incorporated on a cash flow basis. However, these differences should affect the level but not the time pattern of the saving measure. The saving rates are computed as the ratio of the weighted sums of saving and after-tax income. Thus, they reflect the allocation of the average dollar, not the average household.

socioeconomic groups to determine whether saving rates have changed across or within those groups in ways that correspond to changes in the national accounts. Group-specific saving rates, shown in table 4-3, distinguish households by the age of the household head, relative income, homeownership, and education.[15] The most striking aspect is the extent to which the group-specific saving rates all tend to change over the years in roughly parallel fashion, suggesting that the factors responsible for the change in reported saving were common to most households.[16]

In summary, the similarity of the large deteriorations in household saving over the past two decades in Canada and the United States suggests common influences within the two countries. The leading candidate in this regard is the large valuation gains for household wealth in both countries. The increase in home prices was more dramatic in the United States, but both saw substantial increases in the value of corporate equity. Neither country has experienced a significant change in its demographic structure, and real interest rates have been low and falling.

The conflicts arise with regard to the role of Ricardian equivalence and the influence of corporate saving. Both countries achieved major improvements in their fiscal situations in the late 1990s, but Canada sustained its improvement into the 2000s, whereas the United States reverted to a pattern of significant budget deficits. Some Canadian studies emphasize Ricardian equivalence as an important explanation for the decline in household saving. The conflicts arise in that the decline in saving began well before the program of fiscal consolidation and the gains in the wealth-income ratio. Furthermore, the offsetting rise in corporate saving is sufficient to eliminate any evidence of a decline in the private saving rate after 1995.

Japan

Japan has experienced a fall in saving even more dramatic than that of the United States. The household saving rate fell from 12 percent of disposable income in 1980 to 9 percent in 1995 and then plummeted to only 1 percent in 2006–08 before rising back to 3 percent during the financial

15. No information was available on educational attainment in the 1997–2001 surveys.

16. Unfortunately, measurement error is a potential common influence if all households have trouble recalling their expenditures. However, errors in the financial estimate of saving may not be as correlated across households.

Table 4-3. *Canada Group-Specific Saving Rates as a Percent of Disposable Income, 1969–2008*

Category	1969	1978	1982	1986	1992	1997	2001	2005–08
Age								
<30	0.7	3.2	7.2	–0.3	1.0	1.6	4.3	5.9
30–39	2.4	7.1	13.0	5.5	4.9	10.0	10.7	10.2
40–49	4.4	10.3	11.2	7.3	9.1	10.4	11.5	13.1
50–59	6.7	15.1	18.2	12.2	11.7	17.3	15.3	18.5
60+	6.2	16.0	20.3	12.7	10.5	9.7	9.7	11.0
Education								
Less than high school	0.5	7.6	12.3	4.9	3.6			7.1
High school	3.7	8.6	11.6	4.6	4.9			8.6
Some college	4.6	9.2	14.3	8.0	7.7			12.1
College	12.7	19.0	20.7	15.7	15.4			18.6
Marital status								
Single	2.9	7.8	10.1	4.1	1.2	4.5	6.2	5.8
Married	4.2	10.5	14.8	8.5	9.7	12.7	12.8	15.2
Current disposable income quintile								
1	–28.3	–14.7	–9.3	–19.6	–29.1	–36.7	–27.1	–35.6
2	–9.1	–1.3	2.1	–6.5	–4.8	–4.3	–6.4	–6.6
3	–2.4	4.7	7.9	0.2	0.3	2.2	2.8	2.4
4	4.2	10.8	14.3	6.5	7.9	8.3	7.3	10.8
5	16.0	21.8	26.4	20.7	20.9	24.5	24.5	27.7

Sources: Statistics Canada (2011c) and author's calculations.

crisis in 2009.[17] This is a striking development for an economy that once attracted attention for its extraordinarily high saving (Hayashi 1986 and Horioka 1989). At the same time, there have also been major changes in other components of national saving. As shown in table 4-4, a large

17. The measures of net saving from the national accounts are adjusted, as suggested by Hayashi (1986, 1997), by substituting a replacement-cost measure of depreciation for the historical cost basis in order to more closely match international concepts. The adjustment lowers the net household saving rate by about 2 percentage points in the 1980s, but the two concepts have converged in recent years. Nonprofit institutions serving households are also included with the household sector.

Table 4-4. *Japanese Net Saving and Investment by Sector,*
1980–2009[a]

Percent of national disposable income

Item	1980–89	1990–99	2000–08	2009
Saving	16.6	13.2	5.8	–3.1
Government	2.1	1.6	–5.6	–12.9
Private	14.5	11.6	11.4	9.7
Corporate	3.6	2.7	8.9	6.5
Household	10.9	8.9	2.5	3.3
Investment	14.1	10.8	2.7	–4.5
Government	3.4	3.7	0.7	–0.4
Private	10.7	7.2	2.0	–4.0
Corporate	8.3	6.0	2.7	–2.0
Household	2.4	1.1	–0.7	–2.0
Current account	2.5	2.8	4.1	3.5
Statistical discrepancy	0.0	0.6	1.1	2.3

Source: Economic and Social Research Institute (2011).
a. Saving and investment reported net of depreciation measured on a replacement-cost basis.

increase in corporate saving during the past decade offset major portions of the fall in household saving, leaving the private saving rate, which was 14 percent of national income in the 1980s, near 10 percent. Government saving has also changed dramatically, shifting from a positive 2 percent of national income in the 1990s to an average deficit of 6 percent over the last decade. The net effect has been a decline in national saving from 16 percent of national income in the 1980s before the bursting of Japan's asset bubble to 6 percent in 2000–08 and a negative 3 percent in 2009.

The drop in national saving, however, has been matched by an equally large fall in domestic investment (table 4-4), leaving the country with a persistent current account surplus of 3 to 4 percent of national income. Thus, Japan continues to add to its external net worth: foreign net assets have grown to represent over 10 percent of the nation's total wealth, and they are equivalent to 75 percent of national income.[18]

---

18. Currently, Japan is the world's largest creditor nation, with $2.9 trillion of net foreign assets at the end of 2009, and the United States is the largest debtor, with $2.7 trillion of net liabilities. China has $1.8 trillion of net foreign assets.

Figure 4-5. *Inverse of Aged Dependency and Total Saving Rates in Japan, 1980–2010*[a]

Percent of disposable income

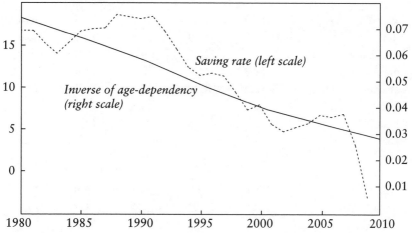

Sources: Economic and Social Research Institute (2011); United Nations (2009); and author's calculations.

a. National saving rate is reported as a percent of national disposable income (see table 4-4); the inverse of the aged dependency rate is the population aged 15–64 years divided by the population age 65 years and older.

The secular fall in household saving has been widely attributed to the rapid aging of the Japanese population.[19] The life-cycle model of household behavior emphasizes the desire of households to smooth lifetime consumption in the presence of a pronounced, hump-shaped age-earnings profile, in which earnings rise up to about age 50–60 and then fall significantly as people prepare for and enter retirement. The model postulates that households will save during their working years to finance their retirement; hence, the saving rate will vary inversely with the ratio of retirees to the working-age population. That relationship is highlighted in figure 4-5, and it would seem to be a very apt description of the general evolution of saving in Japan.

Immediately after World War II, Japan had a very young population, which had the effect of boosting its saving rate. However, due to a sharp fall in the birth rate and increased life expectancy, it is now aging at a

19. Examples are Horioka (1991, 1997, 2010) and Koga (2006).

Table 4-5. *Dependency Rate for Various Countries, 1950–2050*

Region	1950	1975	2000	2010	2050
	Panel A. Aged dependency rate[a]				
Europe[b]	14.5	21.1	24.7	27.6	50.6
Italy	12.4	19.4	27.4	31.3	62.4
Germany	14.5	23.3	24.0	30.9	59.1
United States	12.8	16.3	18.7	19.4	35.1
Canada	12.2	12.9	18.5	20.3	43.4
Japan	8.3	11.6	25.3	35.1	74.3
China	7.2	7.8	10.1	11.4	38.0
India	5.3	6.1	7.0	7.7	20.2
	Panel B. Child dependency rate[a]				
Europe[b]	36.6	37.3	25.2	23.9	26.4
Italy	40.9	38.3	21.3	21.7	25.3
Germany	34.6	33.8	23.0	20.2	22.9
United States	41.7	39.1	32.6	30.3	27.8
Canada	47.4	40.0	27.9	23.5	26.5
Japan	59.3	35.9	21.4	20.5	22.0
China	54.1	70.4	38.1	27.7	24.9
India	63.1	70.7	57.7	47.9	26.8

Source: United Nations (2009).

a. Aged dependency rate is defined as the population over age 64 divided by the working age population (age 15–64). Child dependency rate is defined as the population age 14 and under divided by the population age 15–64 years.

b. Europe comprises Austria, Belgium, Denmark, Finland, France, Germany, Italy, Netherlands, Norway, Spain, Sweden, and the United Kingdom.

very fast rate. The aged dependency rate—the ratio of the population over age 65 to the working population (age 15–64)—has risen very rapidly in recent decades, doubling from 12 percent in 1975 to 25 percent in 2000 and accelerating to 35 percent in 2010 (table 4-5). While the current dependency rate is not that far above that of some European countries such as Germany and Italy, the pace of change has been exceptional.

If the aged do dissave, as postulated by the life-cycle model, the aging of Japan could be a major factor behind the fall in the aggregate saving rate. It is very difficult, however, to measure the saving of the elderly because a significant proportion live in multi-generation households. According to Horioka (2010), 73.4 percent of the elderly lived with their children in 1980 and the proportion was still 49.6 percent in 2005. In addition, prior to 2002 Japan regularly collected data on income, expenditures, and saving only for worker households of two or more persons; thus, it excluded single-person households and households whose head was not working. Horioka shows on the basis of recent data obtained from an expansion of the annual Family Income and Expenditure Survey (FIES) that *retired* aged people who live independently of their children do dissave and that the magnitude of their dissaving has increased since 2000. He interprets these findings as showing that the life-cycle model is highly applicable to the case of Japan.

The controversy about the importance of aging arises from the question of whether the dissaving of retired aged households is enough to account for the large magnitude of decline in the aggregate saving rate. The FIES data indicate little or no decline in saving rates for the average of all Japanese worker households with two or more members, and the retired still account for a relatively small share of overall household income.[20] However, the FIES may be subject to the same problem found in the United States: that households are increasingly prone to under-report their consumption outlays. Still, there would have to be a much larger than indicated difference in saving rates across age cohorts to account for the speed and magnitude of the decline in the overall saving rate.

It is less plausible that variations in wealth have had a significant impact on the household saving rate, because the large rise in the wealth-income ratio took place during the 1980s: an increase from 5.8 times disposable income in 1980 to a peak of 9.7 times in 1989. After the collapse of the asset price bubble, it quickly fell to about 7.5 times disposable income by the mid-1990s, and it has remained roughly stable since then. While the Japanese still have an extraordinary level of wealth by international standards, the large fall in the ratio over the past two decades would have been expected to bolster saving. But those large holdings of liquid assets, combined with little or no growth in incomes, seem instead to have left

20. The saving rate for all worker households averaged 24.7 percent in 1990 and 25.4 percent in 2009. However, the rate of those age 60 and over fell from 19 percent in 1990 to 9 percent in 2009. Furthermore, if the analysis is restricted to those ages 60 and over who are retired, the saving rate fell from –11.5 percent in 1995 to –28.5 percent in 2009. This appears to be the result of a significant decline in their relative incomes rather than a rise in consumption.

Japanese households with little interest in replenishing their wealth after the losses on real estate and share prices.[21]

In sum, the fall in the household saving rate in Japan is similar to that in the United States and Canada, but it is difficult to relate the three to common influences. Japan has had no significant gains in wealth over the past two decades, and it is a leading counterexample in the debate over the importance of Ricardian equivalence. Many Japanese scholars attribute the falloff to the aging of the population, something that is still of little import in the United States and Canada.

The large fall in household saving combined with large deficits in the public sector would seem to leave Japan critically short of saving, but that has not been the case. The major reason is an offsetting surge in corporate saving that began during the worst part of the financial crisis of the early 1990s. The share of corporate profits in national income doubled from an average of 5.5 percent during the boom of the 1980s to more than 10 percent in the middle of the last decade. At the same time, Japanese corporations have maintained their tradition of paying little or no dividends. Given continued low rates of investment, the corporate sector has joined the household sector as a net lender instead of a net user of funds, which was its traditional role.

The overall result has been a remarkable shift in the patterns of saving and investment within the Japanese economy over the past two decades and an extraordinary revision of its economic prospects. It has transitioned from being one of the world's fastest-growing economies to one of the slowest and from being a country famous for its high rate of household saving to having one of the lowest rates among the advanced economies. Furthermore, rates of net investment have been negative in recent years. Many observers believe that the current Japanese situation is unsustainable, but there continues to be a shortage of policy prescriptions. Certainly the demographic trends will persist for the indefinite future.

Europe

The advanced economies of Europe have experienced a significantly smaller drop in national saving as a percent of national income than

21. Horioka (1996) did find a significant wealth effect for the period preceding the collapse of asset prices in the 1990s, but recent studies have placed less emphasis on wealth effects.

Table 4-6. *European Net Saving and Investment by Sector,*
1980–2009
Percent of national disposable income

Item	1980–89	1990–99	2000–04	2005–08	2009
Saving	8.5	8.1	8.0	8.7	3.9
Government	–1.9	–2.5	–0.5	0.4	–5.0
Private	10.5	10.6	8.5	8.3	8.9
Corporate	1.7	2.3	2.7	3.4	2.4
Household	8.7	8.3	5.8	5.0	6.5
Investment	9.2	8.0	7.1	7.8	3.6
Government	1.4	0.9	0.6	0.7	1.0
Private	7.9	7.0	6.4	7.1	2.5

Sources: Organization for Economic Cooperation and Development (2011) and author's calculations.

the United States and Japan; in fact, the German saving rate increased during the 2000s, both because of a rise in the household saving rate and an improved fiscal balance. Rates of net saving for the government, corporate, and household sectors are summarized in table 4-6 for an aggregate of twelve European countries for which data are available back to 1980. The aggregate statistics do show some falloff in household saving over recent decades, but it was fully offset by a sustained pattern of fiscal consolidation up to the 2008–09 financial crisis.[22] Most of the major European countries did have large declines in their rate of national saving prior to 1980. In the aftermath of World War II, emphasis was placed on promoting both public and private saving as part of an effort to rebuild the European economies and catch up to the income levels of the United States. The gradual shift of emphasis away from economic recovery lead to a reduction in national rates of saving, which fell between 1960 and 1980, but the rate of decline has slowed substantially in more recent decades.

There have been a relatively small number of studies focused on the pattern of saving behavior within Europe specifically, but the larger

22. Our sample does not include Greece, Ireland, and Portugal, three of the countries that have been the focus of concern about excessive public sector indebtedness, because of a shortage of reliable historical data. However, Ireland was not a significant debtor prior to the financial crisis.

European countries have been prominent in cross-country studies that focused on common potential influences on saving.[23] Those common factors have included demographic change, the role of wealth changes, and the offsetting private sector responses to fiscal consolidations (Ricardian equivalence).

First, with respect to demographic influences, the European aged dependency rate, which lies between that of the United States and Japan, has been rising for some time, but it does not show the sharp acceleration in recent decades that has occurred in Japan (table 4-5). European aged dependency rates were well above those of Japan in 1975, roughly equivalent in 2000, and significantly below by 2010. The discussion of the effects of demographic change on saving is also more complex in the case of Europe than Japan because of the diversity of the institutional arrangements across countries. According to Börsch-Supan and Lusardi (2003), for example, retirement is unlikely to be a major motive for saving in Germany and Italy because of the generosity of their public pension systems. As contrasting situations, the authors point to the Netherlands and the United Kingdom, with relatively low pension replacement rates. The result is large variations in the age profile of the population across countries with no obvious link to similar changes in rates of saving. They emphasize instead changes in the institutional arrangements, precautionary and bequest motives, and imperfections in capital markets that have limited household borrowing.

There are also significant variations among the European countries in the relative importance of wealth as a determinant of consumption/saving. One of the most recent cross-national studies is Slacalek (2009), which used a panel data set of sixteen countries (twelve of which were located in Europe) to estimate the effects of financial and housing wealth on consumption. It was also possible to distinguish among countries with market- or bank-based financial systems and those with more developed or less developed mortgage markets. He found significant variations in the marginal propensity to consume wealth, ranging from 6 percent in the Anglo-Saxon countries to 4 percent in countries with market-based financial systems and less than 2 percent in countries with bank-based finance and underdeveloped mortgage markets. France, Germany, and Italy were classified with the last group, for which financial wealth had a significant but small effect and housing wealth had no apparent

23. Recent Studies are Hüfner and Koske (2010) and Börsch-Supan and Lusardi (2003).

correlation. While there was some increase in wealth effects in these countries in the 1990s and into 2000s, the run-up of asset prices after the mid-1990s would appear to have had a much smaller impact on saving within continental Europe.

The focus on fiscal consolidation programs in the aftermath of the 2008–09 financial crisis has reenergized the debate over Ricardian equivalence and the magnitude of the private saving offset to changes in fiscal policy. Two European cases, Denmark (1983–86) and Ireland (post-1997), are the two most cited cases in which large-scale fiscal consolidation appeared to stimulate private sector spending. There is recent evidence of a significant private saving offset in a majority of the European economies (Cuaresma and Reitschuler 2007). Furthermore, high levels of public indebtedness are exerting especially negative pressures on several European economies as investors question the sustainability of their fiscal policies. As a result, post-crisis fiscal consolidation has achieved greater emphasis in Europe, with strong expectations that private sector offsets will negate what would otherwise be significant contractionary forces. Many European governments have become strong proponents of Ricardian equivalence, in contrast to the Keynesian views that are more dominant within the United States.

China

Throughout the past quarter-century of rapid economic growth in China, the country has attracted attention for its extraordinary rate of saving. The gross national saving rate averaged 38 percent of GDP in the 1990s and rose to over 50 percent in the last half of the first decade of the 2000s. During most of that period, the high saving was matched by an equally elevated rate of investment. However, in the years after China's 2001 admission to the WTO, the investment rate leveled out, and the saving spilled over into very large trade and current account surpluses with the rest of the world. In a fundamental accounting sense, any excess of saving over domestic investment must be matched by an equal current account surplus; nevertheless, the ease with which the transfer occurred was a surprise, and the magnitude of the resulting current account surplus and its causes have been a focus of international discussion.

Two alternative measures of the Chinese national saving rate are shown in figure 4-6 for the period of 1982–2009. Because the National Bureau of Statistics does not provide estimates of capital consumption

Figure 4-6. *Alternative Measures of National Saving, China, 1982–2009*[a]

Percent of gross national income

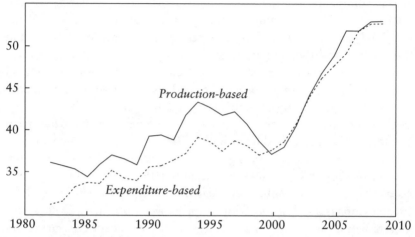

Sources: National Bureau of Statistics of China (2011) and author's calculations.

a. The measures of GNI and GDP by expenditure are from National Bureau of Statistics of China (2011, tables 2-1 and 2-17). Gross saving is GNI minus consumption.

allowances (depreciation), the saving rates are reported on a gross basis as a percentage of gross national income (GNI). The two estimates differ due to variations in the statistical discrepancy between the production-based and expenditure-based measures of GDP, which was quite large in the early 1990s. By either measure, it is evident that China has long had an exceptionally high saving rate by international standards, and it rose sharply during the first decade of the 2000s. Several studies have gone on to document that China's saving rate is an outlier even by the standards of other East Asian economies that reported very high saving rates during their previous episodes of rapid economic growth (Kuijs 2006; Park and Shin 2009). Part of the explanation is the extraordinary pace of overall growth; internationally, there is a strong positive correlation between income growth and the saving rate that results from the lag in adjusting living standards to rapid changes in income. In addition, Ma and Yi (2010) indentifies a number of secular trends and institutional factors that the authors believe have contributed to the high saving rate. They include rapid urbanization, the compressed pace of decline in the child dependency rate, and the growth of private homeownership. In addition, a sustained period of surplus labor and the shedding of excess workers in the state enterprises promoted strong gains in the profits of both public and private enterprises.

Estimates of saving and investment for the major institutional sectors (households, enterprises, and government) are available beginning in 1992. Those measures are shown in table 4-7 as shares of gross national disposable income. While much of the discussion focuses on the saving of Chinese households, it is clear from the table that a large portion of the saving originates with enterprises (public and private) and a consistent government budget surplus (Ma and Yi 2010). In fact, the rise of 15 percentage points in the saving rate between 2000 and 2008 reflects equal contributions from all three sectors, and the saving of enterprises has grown to equal that of households.

Ma and Yi summarize a large volume of research on the sources of the rise in the saving rate over the last decade. They point to a substantial rise in the corporate profit share of GDP with a corresponding decline in the proportion of output going to labor compensation. That presumably reflects the substantial supplies of excess labor and the lack of pressure on wage rates. Restructuring of state-owned enterprises and growth of private firms both were contributing factors. Moreover, the tax burden on corporate profits is modest, and most is retained rather than being distributed as dividend income. By construction, all of the disposable income of corporations is credited to saving—in comparison, the average saving rate for households is about 30 percent—so the shift of income to the corporate sector is a substantial contributor to the rise in aggregate saving.

In addition, the growth in the profit share has contributed to a major fall in the household share of disposable income, which has dropped by 12 percentage points from its peak in 1997 because of the decline in the labor share, reduced interest and dividend income, and lower transfer income.[24] However, despite the fall in its income share, the household sector has raised its average saving rate out of its own disposable income from 28 percent in 2002 to 39 percent in 2008 (not shown), providing a second strong boost to the national saving rate. Arriving at an explanation for that increase, after a decade of relative stability, is a continuing

24. The lower net transfer payments reflect an increase in contributions to the public pension that were instituted after introduction of a new system in 1995. Further details about the changes in the factor income distribution are provided in Aziz and Cui (2007) and Bai and Qian (2009).

Table 4-7. *Chinese Gross Saving and Investment by Sector, 1992–2008*

Percent of gross disposable income

Item	Average			Change	
	1992–2000	2001–08	2008	1992–2000	2000–08
Saving	38.0	46.0	52.3	1.3	14.7
Government	3.5	6.5	8.2	−1.1	4.9
Enterprises	14.4	19.6	21.6	4.9	5.0
Households	20.1	19.8	22.5	−2.5	4.8
Investment	39.5	40.8	43.3	−2.0	7.9
Government	2.8	4.3	4.7	0.9	1.7
Enterprises	29.3	27.6	30.0	−3.9	5.5
Households	7.4	8.8	8.6	1.0	0.8
S-I	−1.6	5.2	9.0	3.3	6.8
Current account	1.4	5.7	9.3	0.4	7.5

Source: National Bureau of Statistics of China (2011, table 2-34).

challenge. None of the factors that are commonly cited as explanations for a high rate of household saving in the past changed significantly in the 2000s. Perhaps the acceleration of enterprise restructuring intensified the precautionary motive and made individual households more aware of the need to save for their own retirement needs (Chamon and Prasad 2008), but it is hard to account for the magnitude of the change.[25]

Finally, government saving rose sharply as a share of national income after 2000, reflecting an improvement in government revenues and a scaling back of the share of GNI devoted to public consumption programs. It included a shift of emphasis toward government investment, particularly in infrastructure, instead of consumption. Some of the higher saving can also be attributed to the buildup of pension fund assets. The success of the investments in infrastructure may enable a shift back to public consump-

25. The 1997 reforms were intended to increase the likelihood that workers would actually get a pension, but they did scale back the magnitude of the promises. Thus, it is possible that households interpreted the reforms as reducing the expected future pension.

tion in areas such as education and health care. That would suggest a reduction in the government component of saving in future years.

India

As India's economic growth has accelerated, rising toward that of East Asia, its rate of national saving has also grown dramatically. Over the past three decades, the gross national saving rate has doubled from an average of 17 percent of GNI in the 1970s to 34 percent in 2005–08.[26] The pattern of increase corresponds closely with the acceleration of GDP growth that began in the late 1980s, but the increases have been especially marked since 2000. While the aggregate saving rate remains far below that of China, it shows a similar pattern of impressive increases. And economic growth in India, as in China, has been largely financed out of domestic saving, even if the rise of saving has not gone so far as to generate the large current account surpluses that marked the Chinese economy in the last half of the first decade of the 2000s.

In the Indian national accounts, total saving is the sum of three separately compiled components: public sector saving, corporate saving, and household (including noncorporate enterprise) saving. The Central Statistical Office can construct reasonably good estimates of public sector saving from budget records. Its measure of corporate saving is obtained from a sample of major corporations' income and balance sheets, maintained by the Reserve Bank of India. Household saving is further divided into two independently estimated components: physical saving and net financial saving. Saving in physical assets is simply set to equal investment of the household sector, which is itself a residual estimate after corporate and government investments are taken into account. The estimate of household financial saving is constructed from flow of funds measures of the net addition to total financial assets less the accumulation of the public and corporate sectors.

The national saving rate and its three components are shown as percentages of GNI for the period 1970–2008 in table 4-8. The overall saving rate has risen dramatically especially since the mid-1980s, and the rate of

26. India does compile estimates of depreciation or capital consumption allowances (CCA) within its national accounts, but I report the data in gross terms to enable an easier comparison with China. CCA has slowly grown from 8 percent of GNI in the early 1980s to 10 percent today.

Table 4-8. *Gross Saving and Investment Balance of India,*
1970–2008[a]

Percent of gross national income

Item	1970–79	1980–89	1990–99	2000–04	2005–08
Saving	17.2	19.1	23.3	27.5	34.3
Government	4.2	3.7	1.6	–0.2	3.1
Private	13.0	15.3	21.7	27.7	31.2
Corporate	1.5	1.8	3.8	4.4	8.2
Household	11.5	13.6	17.9	23.2	23.0
Investment	17.4	20.9	24.7	27.0	35.8
Government	8.6	10.6	8.5	7.0	8.7
Private	9.5	11.4	15.3	19.4	26.2
Corporate	2.6	4.5	7.5	6.6	14.3
Household	6.9	6.8	7.8	12.7	11.9
Valuables			0.8	0.8	1.2
Errors and omissions	–0.8	–1.1	0.8	0.0	–0.3
External investment (S-I)	–0.1	–1.4	–1.4	0.5	–1.5

Source: Central Statistical Office (2010).

a. The data incorporate the new series with a base of 2004–05. The data revision for 2004–05 was interpolated back to 2000–01. The data are reported on an April-March fiscal year and extend through 2008–09. Valuables were incorporated into the national accounts beginning in 1999–2000.

increase accelerated after 2005. Initially, the increase was dominated by major gains in household saving, which grew from a modest 12 percent of GNI in the 1970s to 23 percent in the early part of the first decade of the 2000s. Those funds are available to finance investment in other sectors. Public sector saving was actually negative in the late 1990s and early part of the first decade of the 2000s, but it turned positive in mid-decade until the government shifted to a more stimulative policy during the 2008–09 financial crisis. Corporate saving (retained earnings) grew but remained in the range of 3 to 4 percent of GNI throughout the 1990s. It surged, however, in the first decade of the 2000s, following a pattern that we have observed in several other countries, particularly China and Japan. It is now approaching 10 percent of GNI.

Investment, shown in the lower portions of table 4-8, has followed a pattern similar to that of saving, with modest increases in the 1990s and a sharp acceleration during the first decade of the 2000s. That parallelism has kept domestic saving and investment in close balance, and India has fluctuated between modest current account surpluses and deficits. India is also notable for the extent to which the acceleration of output growth preceded the rise in rates of saving and investment (Mishra 2006). The rapid income growth appears to be a primary cause of the rise in saving, rather than the reverse. In addition, the stage of demographic change in India is currently very favorable to economic growth and a rise in rates of saving: the falling birth rate has lowered the rate of child dependency well before any projected rise in aged dependency. It is also noteworthy that foreign investment has increased dramatically from only 1 percent of GDP in 1999–2000 to over 5 percent in 2008–09, becoming an important source of financing and a stimulus to growth. It is a reflection of the greatly improved opportunities for economic growth in India.

Athukorala and Sen (2004) attributed the early portion of the rise in private saving predominantly to increases in the level and rate of growth of income. The authors also found a positive association with the spread of banking facilities and inflation and a substantial inverse correlation with government budget deficits (Ricardian equivalence).

India's saving has evolved in a process that has reduced concerns that it would be a constraint on future growth. The strong rise in private saving is reminiscent of China's previous experience. India is now attracting much higher rates of foreign saving, and there are still major opportunities to improve the fiscal performance of the public sector. Nor is there significant evidence of heightened competition for domestic capital. Nominal interest rates are generally high in India, but inflation is also elevated and often very volatile because of the strong role of commodity prices. Therefore, over the past decade, the estimated real interest rate (the bank lending rate less the rate of wholesale price inflation) has fluctuated over a wide range, but it displays little evidence of a secular increase.

Conclusion

The international comparisons presented above highlight the diversity of experiences with national saving and its components across the globe. Given the variation in saving rates and their trends, it is difficult to conclude that they can be explained in the context of one or two conceptual models. Instead, saving behavior appears to be influenced in important ways by country-specific institutional factors together with a few common determinants, such as income growth, demographic changes, and variations in private wealth. The extent to which some frequently cited factors do not appear as major determinants is also striking. Interest rates are sometimes statistically significant, but with varying signs. The level of income, beyond a low-income minimum, also appears to have only a weak association with the saving rate; while rich households may save more than the poor, the same is clearly not true in a comparison of rich and poor countries.

Moreover, the increase in corporate saving, sufficient in some cases to offset most of the decline in household saving, is a surprisingly large and common characteristic of the last decade. It is due primarily to a rise in the corporate profit rate, but it has been augmented by the general decline in interest costs. Undoubtedly, a portion of the rise in capital's share of income can be attributed to the rise in the prices of primary commodities with their small labor share, but in a broader context there has been considerable debate over the extent to which the rise in the profit share reflects the globalization of labor or technological innovations. In 2007 the IMF published an estimate of the effective global supply of labor and argued that it had quadrupled between 1980 and 2005.[27] Despite the magnitude of the estimated growth in the global labor supply, the IMF study argues that technological change rather than globalization had the largest effect in reducing labor's share and increasing the return to capital.[28]

27. The IMF estimated the effective global supply of labor by weighting each country's labor force by its ratio of exports to GDP (IMF 2007).

28. The effects of globalization were assumed to operate through export and import prices, and the effects of technological change were represented as changes in the capital-labor ratio.

CHAPTER FIVE

Consequences
of Low Saving

How troubled should we be about the decline in saving? To begin, there are several broad areas of concern. First, at the level of the total economy, saving has long been seen as a primary determinant of a nation's capacity to finance investment. Thus, low rates of saving have been associated with depressed rates of capital accumulation and inadequate rates of economic growth. Low saving is also considered dangerous to U.S. economic interests, because it implies an unwelcome reliance on foreign capital flows, which has been associated with financial instability in many other countries. However, these concerns relate primarily to low rates of national saving. Aside from the national concerns, are there reasons to be concerned about the saving of individual households? Most of the attention to household saving has focused on the adequacy of preparations for retirement. Low saving over a lifetime implies a lack of wealth and resources to support retirement. And even at younger ages, low wealth holdings leave people vulnerable to economic shocks such as illness, unemployment, or similar unexpected losses.

The perceived threats, however, have not emerged in the expected ways. The nation has been through a very severe financial crisis and a deep recession, but it is difficult to attribute it to a shortage of saving. Instead of experiencing capital shortages, rising interest rates, and weak economic growth, the U.S. economy performed well in the years before the financial crisis. Credit was readily available, and stronger-than-expected capital accumulation and productivity gains contributed to substantial economic growth. High rates of investment were made possible by the ability to borrow in a global capital market where an apparent surplus of saving actually led to unusually low interest rates. And, thus far, the capital inflows have proven to be far more sustainable than previously anticipated. Similarly, at the household level, there is little evidence that today's retirees are in worse economic circumstances than in the past. The fall in saving was, until the financial crisis, more than offset by capital gains on housing and financial assets. Compared with prior generations, baby boomers appeared to be relatively well prepared for retirement. This chapter explores the implications of low saving in greater detail.

Saving and Capital Formation

A robust and growing economy is the product of many factors, including a skilled workforce and institutions that support rapid technological innovation, but capital accumulation has long been assigned a primary role because new capital often embodies many of the latest, more efficient technologies and it is a primary determinant of the economy's productive capacity. In earlier decades, domestic saving was critical to the process of capital accumulation because countries could obtain only relatively small amounts of financing from overseas sources. Hence, the nation's rate of capital accumulation was tied to its rate of public and private saving. From that perspective, it would seem that thirty years of depressed rates of private saving and public sector budget deficits would have dragged down the nation's rate of capital formation and economic growth. Yet it is hard to discern a linkage between reduced saving and the slowing of economic growth in the recent macroeconomic experience of the United States.

A summary of post–World War II trends in the major sources of U.S. economic growth is shown in table 5-1. The growth in potential (full-employment) output in the nonfarm business sector is separated according to the contributions of increased labor inputs, capital services, and total factor productivity.[1] The most significant slowing of economic growth occurred in the aftermath of the 1973 oil crisis and subsequent recession, but it was concentrated initially in a sharply lower rate of increase in total factor productivity and, beginning in the 1990s, in a falloff in the growth of the labor force. It is notable, however, that the contribution of capital services remained at a stable and high level, averaging in excess of

---

1. The growth accounts are constructed and published annually by the Congressional Budget Office as part of its measure of potential GDP. Potential output is adjusted to exclude cyclical fluctuations.

Table 5-1. *Contributions to the Growth of Potential Output in the Nonfarm Business Sector, 1949–2010*
Annual percentage rates of change

Period	Potential output	Potential hours worked	Capital services	Potential total factor productivity
1949–73	4.0	0.9	1.1	1.9
1973–80	3.7	1.6	1.2	0.9
1980–90	3.2	1.2	1.2	0.7
1990–2000	3.4	0.8	1.3	1.2
2000–08	3.0	0.4	1.0	1.6
2008–10	2.1	0.5	0.5	1.1

Source: Congressional Budget Office (2011, table 2-2).

1 percent a year until the end of the dotcom bubble in 2000.[2] Therefore, in this simple accounting for the contributions to economic growth, there is little evidence of a shortfall of capital accumulation.

The sustained growth of the capital input is the result of two major economic changes. The first change was a large shift in the composition of capital investment toward information technology (IT). The extraordinarily rapid rate of technological innovation in semiconductors and other computer components sharply lowered their cost and greatly stimulated investments in all forms of IT capital. As the price of computing power fell, nominal expenditures on IT capital rose from 1 percent of private fixed investment in 1960 to 10 percent in 1980 and 30 percent by 2000. Adjusted for the price declines, the real value of IT investments grew at a spectacular rate of nearly 20 percent a year between 1980 and 2000. Even though the nominal value of total investment remained relatively stable as a share of GDP, the shift toward IT capital implied strong growth of the real value (adjusted for price changes), outpacing the growth in GDP by a substantial magnitude, particularly during the 1990s. These developments are shown in figure 5-1, which displays private gross investment

2. Capital services refer to the gross flow of productive services from the stock of physical capital, and its rental price is defined by $P_k^s = (i + \delta - \dot{P}_k) \times P_k$, where i represents the rate of return, δ the rate of depreciation, and $\dot{P}_k$ the rate of expected price change of the capital good.

Figure 5-1. *Trends in Nominal and Real Private Investment, 1960–2010*[a]

Percent of GDP

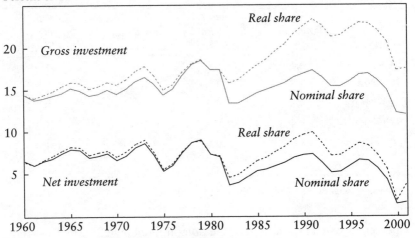

Sources: Bureau of Economic Analysis (2011a, tables 1.1.5 and 1.1.3) and author's calculations.
a. The real values are converted to a base year of 1980.

as a share of GDP in both nominal and real terms for the period of 1960 to the present. Fixed investment was a slowly rising share of GDP in the 1960s and 1970s, but the IT sector was too small to have a major effect on the evolution of the total. Nominal investment fell as a share of GDP throughout the 1980s, from a peak of 18.5 percent in 1979 to 13.5 percent in 1992, before recovering to 17 percent by 2000. However, the strong growth of IT investments and the fall in their price had a more dominant effect on the price-adjusted measure, which was a much higher share of GDP. However, the rapid pace of technical change also implied that the new capital quickly became obsolete, a phenomenon that is captured in a rise in the rate of depreciation. The measures of net investment are also shown in figure 5-1, where it is clear that the more rapid obsolescence offsets substantial portions of the higher gross investment and adds to the evidence of a slowing of capital accumulation after the bursting of the tech bubble in 2000 and its complete collapse in the aftermath of the financial crisis.

The second major development was the emergence of the ability to borrow on a large scale from the rest of the world. Reliance on foreign

Figure 5-2. *Foreign and Domestic Financing of Net Investment,*
1980–2010

Percent of GDP

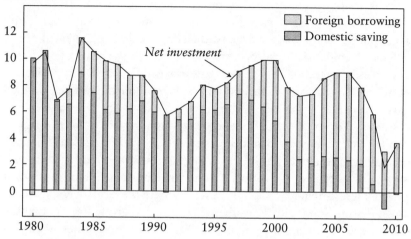

Source: Bureau of Economic Analysis (2011a, tables 5.1 and 1.7.5).

financing first emerged in the early-1980s, when a large budget deficit
and extraordinarily high interest rates attracted large capital inflows
from abroad and drove the real exchange rate to unprecedented levels.
The high value of the dollar in turn weakened U.S. exports and raised
imports. The result was a substantial current account deficit, or net inflow
of foreign resources. As shown in figure 5-2, foreign borrowing financed
about one-third of net investment in 1984–87. The foreign inflows slowed
over the last half of the 1980s in the face of much lower domestic investment demand and interest rates, and the exchange rate returned to its
1980 value. Net foreign saving was negligible in the 1991 recession. It is
notable, however, that the government debt issues of the 1980s were all
denominated in dollars, and when the exchange rate fell over the last half
of the decade, the capital losses were borne by foreign lenders.

The 1990s marked a strong recovery of investment fueled by the expansion of IT spending, and foreign saving reemerged as a significant source
of financing near the end of the decade. When private saving fell in the
latter years of the boom, the foreign share grew to over 50 percent of the
total. Investment spending temporarily slowed in the 2001 recession, but
its recovery was accompanied by even lower rates of domestic saving and
the foreign share of its financing rose further, to over two-thirds of net

investment for the remainder of the 2000s. Ultimately, the net national saving rate turned negative in the aftermath of the financial crisis, and the continued large foreign inflows are vivid evidence that domestic investment is no longer constrained by the volume of national saving.

In summary, despite two decades of low rates of private saving and large public sector budget deficits, the supply side of the United States economy remained surprisingly strong right up to the onset of the financial crisis in late 2008. The boom in domestic demand within the United States continued to generate good investment opportunities, and foreign savers have been more than willing to provide financing when Americans were not. For much of the period, other high-income countries lacked similar investment opportunities, and the 1997–98 regional financial crisis in Asia resulted in much lower rates of investment and a substantial surplus of saving over investment. Thus, there was a fortunate melding of global interests that sustained U.S. investment in the face of very low rates of domestic saving. However, there has been a sharp falloff in potential output growth in the recession, both because of lower rates of capital accumulation and slower total factor productivity growth (table 5-1).

External Imbalances

The progressive integration of the global economy has gone a long way toward severing the link between national saving and domestic investment, but that does not mean that the macroeconomic costs of low saving have vanished. In order to sustain its investment in the face of falling rates of saving, the United States has borrowed large sums from abroad and sold off a substantial portion of its assets. That has changed the nature of the costs, but it has not eliminated them. Within three decades, the United States went from being the world's largest creditor nation to its largest debtor. Many observers worry about the sustainability of the buildup of foreign indebtedness and the burden that it places on future generations.

Much of the debate and confusion surrounding the sources and consequences of the U.S. external imbalance is due to the different perspectives from which it can be analyzed. First, from the domestic side, the external (current account) balance is the difference between the nation's total income and its total expenditures; therefore a deficit can be said to be the result of the nation spending more than it earns and borrowing from the rest of the world and thereby living beyond its means. In a contrasting perspective that emphasizes external relationships, the current account is also defined as the difference between the income earned on exports and other transactions with the rest of the world and payments to foreigners for imports and other services.[3] Thus, just as the current account balance is the result of a net balance between saving and investment on the domestic side, it reflects a netting of earnings from exports less expenditures on imports from the external view. The dominant role of exports and imports leads to a natural focus on the determinants of trade with other countries, such as exchange rates and the relative openness of markets. It also often leads to claims of "unfair" foreign trade practices.

As emphasized in the accounting identities in chapter 2, the two definitions are differing sides of the same phenomenon, but they lead to sharply contrasting public viewpoints on the sources of a current account deficit. Even though the focus herein is on the domestic aspects, it is useful to review the imbalance from both perspectives, recognizing the interactions and the importance of both sets of factors. Moreover, the issues are inherently global because of a third requirement, that national imbalances must be offset on a global basis; thus the current account deficits of some countries are matched by surpluses of others.

Figure 5-3 shows the evolution of the U.S. external balance over the past three decades. The balance of net resource flows as measured by the current account is shown in panel A, and the cumulative net international investment (stock) position of the United States is shown in panel B. As panel A makes clear, there have been two episodes of large current account deficits: that in the early 1980s and the current episode, which emerged in the aftermath of the Asian financial crisis and has resulted in much larger and longer-lasting deficits. Panel A also shows the recent beginning of a correction of the imbalance after 2006, although it has been exaggerated in recent years by the effects of the economic crisis.

Shown in panel B is the cumulative effect of a quarter-century of current account deficits. The United States began with a strong net creditor position exceeding 15 percent of national income in 1980, but its international investment position had plummeted to a negative 25 percent of national income by the end of 2010. It is noteworthy, however, that the balance sheet has not deteriorated as much as would be expected

3. The current account is the sum of three main kinds of external transactions: trade in goods and services, net factor income receipts, and net transfer receipts. Most discussions of external economic relations focus on trade flows because they are the largest component.

Figure 5-3. *U.S. External Balance, 1970–2010*[a]

Percent of national income

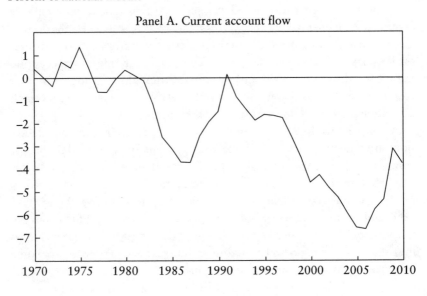

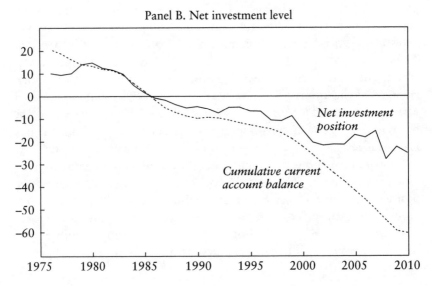

Sources: Bureau of Economic Analysis (2011b, table 2) and Bureau of Economic Analysis (2011a, table 4.1).

a. The net investment position is based on direct investments at current value; the cumulative balance is benchmarked to the net investment position at the end of 1979.

given the large current account imbalances of the last decade. This is shown in panel B by cumulating the current account deficits since 1980 and expressing the result as a share of national income. Annual current account deficits in the range of 4 to 6 percent of national income should translate into a net deterioration of the investment balance of similar magnitudes. Thus, the net indebtedness of the United States would have been expected to exceed 50 percent of national income by 2010. The large difference between the two measures reflects the valuation gains on U.S. investments abroad, which were greater than those on foreign investments in the United States. U.S.-based investors devote large portions of their portfolios to equity-type assets, whereas foreign investors in the United States place greater emphasis on debt instruments. While capital gains and losses are excluded in the official balance of payments accounts, they are included in the balance sheet measures. Furthermore, it is important to note that net foreign ownership still accounts for a small share of the nation's total wealth. As mentioned in chapter 2, total wealth is about five times national income, so that the foreign share of the total is about 5 percent.

Domestic Perspective

It is notable that for most of the past three decades the growing U.S. trade deficit has been associated with a buoyant domestic economy, rapid job growth, and a decline of unemployment to unprecedented levels. This domestic strength suggests that the trade deficit was not something forced on the U.S. economy by outside pressures; rather, it was a response to changing domestic economic conditions that pushed aggregate demand beyond the nation's productive capacity.[4] The excess demand was accommodated in a noninflationary way by exporting less and importing more.

The domestic origins of the current account deficits are evident in the steadily rising share of GDP devoted to consumption. After several decades of stability, private consumption rose from 62 percent of GDP in the 1970s to 70 percent in the 2000s. The growing emphasis on private consumption is the secular domestic counterpart to the growing trade

4. If the deficit were the result of foreign production being unfairly dumped into the U.S. economy, we would expect ongoing problems of excess unemployment and job shortages, something that was not evident prior to the financial crisis. Moreover, the financial crisis clearly had its origins in the United States.

deficit. Even the two episodes of marked reduction in the trade deficit—that in the late 1980s and the current episode—are both notable for being associated with reductions in domestic investment, not a scaling back of consumption.

When a large current account deficit first emerged in the early 1980s, it was in response to a sharp drop in national saving that could be traced in turn to the large budget deficits of the Reagan era. In fact, the simultaneous emergence of a large federal budget deficit and a current account deficit gave rise to an emphasis on the "twin deficits."[5] The two were viewed as linked through the financial pressures of financing a large budget deficit, which led to higher U.S. interest rates, foreign financial inflows, appreciation of the real exchange rate, and a trade deficit. However, the reemergence of a large current account deficit in the late 1990s, despite a rapidly improving fiscal situation, suggested that the notion of a special link between government budget deficits and the external balance was overly simplistic. Instead, the gap between saving and investment in the later years can be traced to a large drop in the private saving rate—due in turn to sharply lower rates of household saving—and strong investment demand.

The 2008–09 economic crisis has brought on another major realignment: household saving has shown a modest increase, but investment demand has collapsed. Moreover, government budget deficits have reemerged during the current decade as a significant contributor to the low national saving rate, and extraordinary fiscal actions in 2008–09 turned the national saving rate negative.

External Perspective

Trade in goods and services constitutes the largest component of the current account. The basic trends in exports and imports, as a percent of GDP, are shown in figure 5-4. Both have been growing over the years as the global economy has become more integrated, and imports received an added impetus from the growing reliance on imported petroleum. Imports have also come to exceed exports by a wide margin, consistent with the large current account imbalance. In a simple summary form, the

5. The linkage between the two deficits is emphasized in Feldstein (1985), but the popular use of the term "twin deficits" seems to have originated earlier and was used, for example, by Paul Volcker in congressional testimony in early 1984 (Volcker 1984).

Figure 5-4. *United States Exports and Imports, 1970–2010*

Percent of national income

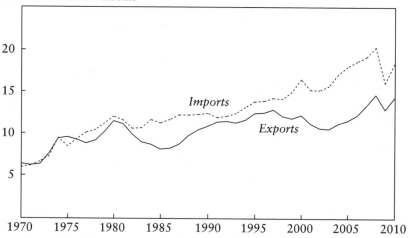

Source: Bureau of Economic Analysis (2011a, table 4.1).

trade balance is driven by rates of growth in foreign incomes (Y_f) relative to rates of growth in domestic incomes (Y_d) and the price of domestic-produced goods relative to that of foreign-produced goods (q):

(1) $$NX = f(Y_f, Y_d, q)$$

Rapid growth in domestic incomes raises the demand for imports, and growth in foreign markets has a similar effect on exports. The concept of the real exchange rate provides a simple measure of relative prices; it is defined as the nominal exchange rate (e) multiplied by the ratio of foreign and domestic prices (P_d/P_f):[6]

(2) $$q = e \times (P_d/P_f)$$

Thus, a rise in the real exchange rate raises the foreign price of U.S. exports and lowers the domestic cost of imports, leading to deterioration in the trade balance.

6. The exchange rate is measured as the foreign price of domestic currency; appreciation of the currency is recorded as an increase in the exchange rate index.

Figure 5-5. *Alternative Measures of the Real Exchange Rate, 1975–2010*

Index (2000 = 100)

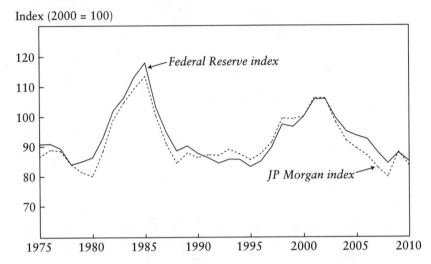

Sources: Board of Governors of the Federal Reserve (2011b), and JPMorgan (2011).

Two alternative measures of the U.S. real exchange rate are shown in figure 5-5. Both are weighted averages of exchange rates with major trading partners, with weights based on bilateral trade flows, and an appreciation of the dollar is shown as a rise in the index. The Federal Reserve reports a measure that uses consumer price indexes to adjust for differential rates of price change, while JPMorgan publishes an index that is based on producer price indexes for manufacturing goods, excluding food and fuels. The two measures show very similar movements, with a large appreciation of the exchange rates in the early 1980s and a return to the historical level over the last half of the decade.[7] A second cycle is evident in a rise in the exchange rate in the last half of the 1990s up to about 2002, followed by another period of correction. There was also a surge in the dollar's value in the midst of the financial crisis, as investors sought the safety of U.S. Treasury securities.

The real exchange rate also shows a very strong negative correlation with the current account balance: a currency appreciation is associated

7. An advantage of the JPMorgan index is that comparable measures are provided for all of the major trading economies.

Figure 5-6. *Correlation of the Non-Oil Trade Balance and the Real Exchange Rate, 1980–2010*

Trade balance as a percent of GDP

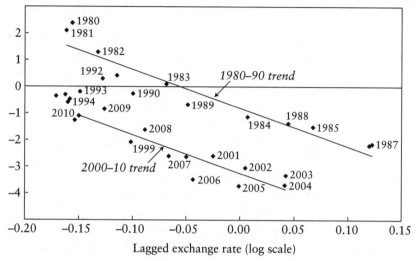

Lagged exchange rate (log scale)

Sources: Bureau of Economic Analysis (2011a, table 4.1); Board of Governors of the Federal Reserve (2011b); and author's calculations.

with a deteriorating current account balance. However, it is also true that there is a substantial lag in the effect of the exchange rate on trade flows because it takes time for exporters and importers to adjust to their changed competitive positions. A simple means of summarizing the relationship is provided in figure 5-6, which graphs the non-oil trade balance against a three-year weighted average of the exchange rate.[8] While trade is affected by other factors, after lags are accounted for, the exchange rate plays a fundamental role. There is also evidence that the trade balance has been deteriorating over time irrespective of the real exchange rate. The implication is that restoration of the external balance would require a major fall in the real exchange rate because that is the only short-term means of raising the competitiveness of U.S. exports. While some of the

8. The non-oil trade balance is measured as a percent of GDP, and the exchange rate is a weighted average of the Federal Reserve Bank index, with weights of .25, .5, and .25 on the rates, lagged one, two, and three years. The figure is based on an earlier presentation in Baily and Lawrence (2006).

decline from the 2002 peak has already occurred, most studies suggest that a return to trade balance would require still further price change.

Why is the large external deficit a problem? After all, if the rest of the world wishes to finance overconsumption by the United States, why should we complain? Given the domestic desire to forego saving as part of a societal turn toward consumption, the inflow of foreign saving provides a means of financing a large portion of the nation's investment that would otherwise have been forgone. Thus, it is seen by some as an effective second-best approach to maintaining the productivity of the economy.

Yet there are reasons for concern.[9] First, the deterioration of the U.S. international investment position generates concerns about a risk of a "hard landing" in which a shift in investor confidence causes a plunge in the dollar, a surge in interest rates, and a recession. Such crises of confidence have been a problem in other countries, and foreign investors might become unwilling to tolerate further exposure to U.S. markets. While the United States is still viewed as central to the world economy and risk premiums on its debts remain extremely low, reputation is an amorphous concept; once lost, it may prove difficult to regain.[10] Also, the sheer magnitude of the budget deficit and the dysfunctional response of the political system to it led Standard & Poors to downgrade the AAA rating of U.S. government bonds in August 2011.

Second, in the aftermath of the financial crisis, the nature of the debate has changed. The United States is no longer a high-employment society debating the wisdom of liquidating a portion of its wealth to support consumption. The household saving rate has recovered as individuals seek to rebuild their wealth position, and the problem has become a deficiency of demand and a shortage of jobs. A policy of pumping up household income with tax reductions and high government transfer payments is increasingly hard to sustain. The problems have been made even more difficult by the collapse of the prior investment opportunities that motivated

9. Differing perspectives and discussions on the sustainability of current account deficits are found in Bertaut, Kamin, and Thomas (2009), Cline (2005), Edwards (2005), and Obstfeld and Rogoff (2004).

10. Paradoxically, the crisis that emerged in 2008 seems more related to a surplus of capital inflows than to any shortage, and the dollar surged in value with the onset of the crisis. Some observers now perceive the crisis to have been the result of the excessive willingness of foreigners to allocate funds to the United States, which in turn contributed to a series of speculative bubbles in U.S. asset markets.

much of the foreign capital inflow. The current overhang of real estate capital may take many years to be fully absorbed.[11] The nation therefore needs the jobs that would be created by shifting its productive resources into exports, which would lead to a more balanced international trade position. In this respect, the trade deficit and an overvalued dollar were especially damaging to the tradable goods sector, wherein many U.S. corporations have become foreign in all but name, having shifted a preponderance of their production facilities to more competitive locations.

Third, the ease with which the nation can borrow internationally, combined with the myopia exhibited by voters and their representatives, has greatly complicated the debate over public sector budgets. The discussion has long been framed by the notion of a budget constraint—recognition that expenditures would be limited by tax revenues—and the benefits of additional programs had to be balanced against the costs of higher taxes. Yet in a vast global financial market, the third option of continuing to borrow the funds from abroad is seen as nearly costless. Therefore most voters respond to polls by voicing support for current programs and opposition to any tax increases to pay for them. Policymakers advocate fiscal deficits as a form of fiscal stimulus or job creation, but in an open global economy, much of the stimulus will flow abroad.

Adequacy of Retirement Saving

The adequacy of household saving, with respect to both precautionary saving in the face of adverse short-run shocks (unemployment or health problems) and the longer-term needs of retirement, has long been an area of public policy concern and research. Expressions of concern have been especially frequent since the fall in saving began in the 1980s. Bernheim was one of the first to argue that large portions of the baby boom population were saving less than they should to meet retirement needs (Bernheim 1991). Similar concerns have been expressed more recently in Munnell, Webb, and Golub-Sass (2007).

---

11. Congressional Budget Office (2008) suggested that the underlying demand for new housing units was about 1.5 million. That contrasts with a 2011 level of starts of about 600,000. Yet most forecasters perceive little significant growth over the next few years due to continuing financial problems.

Incomes of the Aged

There is however, surprisingly little evidence of a growing problem. The annual Current Population Surveys (CPS) suggest that the incomes of those over the age of 65 grew much faster than the incomes of the non-elderly between 1970 and 1990 and have grown at roughly equal rates since then.[12] Similarly, the poverty rate among the elderly has fallen sharply since 1970, and today it is equivalent to the rate for those aged 18–64 and substantially below the rate for children.

Some of the reasons for the lack of a correlation between the saving rate and the economic well-being of the elderly emerge from an analysis of the composition of their income. Table 5-2 reports the major sources of income for the aged (65 +) by quintiles of total income for 1990 and 2008.[13] The 1990 data were chosen for the comparison because the working life of 1990 retirees largely predates the decline in saving.

To begin, the distribution of total income received by elderly households is reported in the second column of the table. Social Security pensions are the largest single source, accounting for 37 percent of the total in 2008. Income from savings (pensions and own assets) represents 31 percent, earnings from wages and self-employment for a surprisingly large 30 percent, and the remainder, 3 percent, consists largely of various public assistance programs. The only significant changes in the sources of income of the aged since 1990 are a large 12 percentage point fall in the share of asset income, offset by an equivalent rise in the share derived from earnings. The diminished importance of asset income can be traced largely to the steady fall in interest rates over the past two decades, but the percentage of aged persons reporting any asset income also peaked at 70 percent in 1990 and sank to 55 percent by 2008.[14] The CPS does not include income from capital gains, nor does it reflect the progressive sale

12. Median real household income of households with a household head or spouse age 65 and over rose by 61 percent between 1970 and 1990; the comparable rate for all households was 16 percent. Between 1990 and 2008, growth was lower for both, 18 and 10 percent, respectively.

13. The data are from the annual CPS; they include both married couples in which one member is over age 65 and single persons.

14. Fisher (2007) did find that an increasing proportion of respondents to the SCF are likely to report no asset income despite holding assets that would normally involve such payments. However, the under-reporting is concentrated in those with very small holdings.

Table 5-2. *Percentage of the Income of Aged Households from Specified Source, by Quintile of Money Income, 1990 and 2008*

Source	Total	Income quintile				
		1	2	3	4	5
1990						
Social Security	37.2	79.7	77.0	60.1	42.6	18.6
Government and private pensions	17.5	3.0	6.6	14.7	21.3	19.7
Earnings	17.7	0.8	2.9	7.1	12.4	26.7
Income from assets	24.5	4.0	8.5	14.8	21.0	33.0
Cash assistance/other	3.1	12.6	5.0	3.4	2.7	2.1
	100.0	100.0	100.0	100.0	100.0	100.0
2008						
Social Security	36.8	83.6	82.3	65.0	43.9	18.0
Government and private pensions	18.2	2.9	7.0	15.8	25.2	18.6
Earnings	29.7	1.8	3.9	9.8	19.4	43.7
Income from assets	12.7	2.1	3.4	6.5	8.4	17.8
Cash assistance/other	2.7	9.6	3.4	2.8	3.0	1.9
	100.1	100.0	100.0	100.0	100.0	100.0
Difference						
Social Security	–0.4	3.9	5.3	4.9	1.3	–0.6
Government and private pensions	0.7	–0.1	0.4	1.1	3.9	–1.1
Earnings	12.0	1.0	1.0	2.7	7.0	17.0
Income from assets	–11.8	–1.9	–5.1	–8.3	–12.6	–15.2
Cash assistance/other	–0.4	–3.0	–1.6	–0.6	0.3	–0.2

Source: U.S. Social Security Administration (2011).

of financial assets to support consumption, but the rise in the percentage of aged households with no asset income suggests that fewer households had been accumulating savings for retirement. Furthermore, the CPS does not include the income from defined contribution plans and the rollover of funds from pension accounts into IRAs. The slower growth in asset income, however, has been fully offset by increases in the earned income of the elderly, and we do not know the extent to which the increase in earned income is a reaction to the loss of asset income.

The aggregation of the income of all aged households, however, is potentially misleading in its focus on the average dollar instead of on a representative range of individuals. There are large differences in the composition of the sources of income for individuals at the top and bottom of the income distribution. This feature is highlighted in the other columns of table 5-2. The lower two quintiles, 40 percent of the aged population, rely on Social Security for over 80 percent of their income, and income from savings amounts to less than 10 percent. Thus, for practical purposes, those quintiles do not have significant savings. Even in the third quintile, Social Security accounts for 65 percent of total income. Only in the top two quintiles of the aged does income from savings (pensions and own assets) represent a significant portion of the total. In effect, retirement appears to have been an important motivation for saving only for those at the top of the income distribution Despite the differences in the sources of their income, aged households at the bottom and top of the distribution experienced similar rates of increase in the 1990s. During the 2000s, however, there was a widening of the distribution because those at the top of the distribution had somewhat larger gains.[15]

Retirement Wealth

Most studies of the adequacy of preparedness for retirement have focused on the accumulation of savings before retirement relative to some standard of needs. The most straightforward measures compare the financial condition of those entering retirement with that of prior generations. Data on wealth holdings are available from the Survey of Consumer Finances (SCF) for the period of 1983 to 2007. As shown in figure 5-7, low rates of saving did not result in a deteriorating household wealth position over the interval of 1983 to 2007. Adjusted for inflation, net wealth was either stable or increasing at all ages. In this respect, the SCF is fully consistent with the discussion in chapter 3 in indicating that, at least up to the financial crisis, capital gains on housing and financial assets had more than offset the cumulative effects of reduced rates of saving. The picture may be a bit too favorable in that incomes, and thus expectations of retirement well-being, have also increased. Age-specific wealth-income ratios are reported in the bottom panel, but those are also stable or rising over time. An additional analysis examined the wealth-income

15. Income at the break between the first and second quintiles rose by 41 percent between 1990 and 2000, while it rose by 38 percent for the break between the fourth and fifth quintiles. In the 2000s the changes were 30 percent and 41 percent, respectively.

Figure 5-7. *Wealth in the Survey of Consumer Finances, by Age*

Panel A. Real wealth (thousands of 2000 dollars)

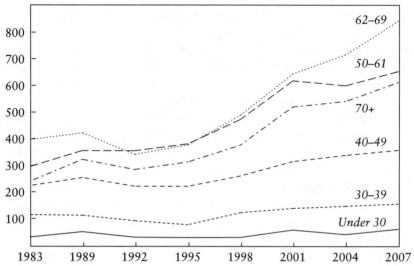

Panel B. Wealth-income ratio

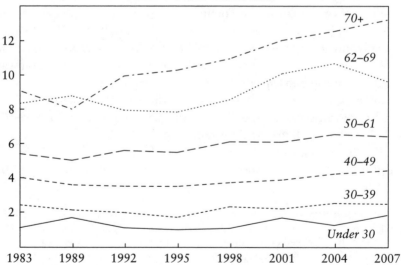

Sources: Bureau of Economic Analysis (2011b, table 2) and Bureau of Economic Analysis (2011a, table 4.1).

a. The net investment position is based on direct investments at current value; the cumulative balance is benchmarked to the net investment position at the end of 1979.

ratios by income levels and education as well as age, but except among the youngest members of the low-income groups, there is little evidence of significant deterioration of wealth holdings.[16]

More comprehensive evaluations of retirement adequacy attempt to project retirement needs relative to pre-retirement consumption as a means of defining a replacement percentage of pre-retirement income. Conceptually, it is a useful refinement, but it has proved difficult to define retirement needs because of significant changes in consumption patterns around the time of retirement. In addition, the conversion from measures of wealth to retirement income requires an assumption about the terms on which individuals can purchase annuities.[17] In practice, many households do not convert their wealth to annuities, preferring to self-insure against mortality risk, but the concept is useful for translating wealth to income equivalents.

The price of an annuity has increased both because today's retirees are expected to live longer and because the interest rate has fallen. Life expectancy at age 65 has increased by about 10 percent over the past twenty-five years, and long-term interest rates have declined from about 8 percent in 1989–91 to 4 percent in 2008–10. That alone would translate into a reduction of 25 to 30 percent in the value of an annuity for a 65-year-old male. However, because a lower expected rate of inflation accounts for about half of the fall in the nominal interest rate, the reduction in an inflation-indexed real annuity would be substantially less.[18] Until very recently, however, it was not possible to purchase insurance against the combination of longevity risk and inflation; that form of protection was available only in public pensions. Still, even a crude measure of the cost of an inflation-indexed annuity suggests that the wealth-income ratio would need to have risen substantially over the past two decades to leave the elderly equally well prepared for retirement.

A 2003 assessment of a large number of research reports on retirement preparedness concluded that most baby boomers were likely to be

16. A more detailed analysis of the SCF data is provided in Gale and Pence (2006).

17. There has been a substantial fall in the direct receipt of annuity income due to the shift from defined benefit to defined contribution pensions. There has been an increase, however, in the private purchase of annuities as an investment vehicle. Developments in annuity markets are discussed in Brown and others (2001).

18. It is difficult to obtain an accurate measure of the change in real interest rates because until recently the market for inflation-indexed bonds was very illiquid. However, adjustments of nominal interest rates, using surveys of inflation expectations, suggest a fall of about 3 percent over the past quarter-century (see chapter 4 of this volume).

better off in retirement than their predecessors (Congressional Budget Office 2003). However, the report recognized that reduced reliance on annuitized income increased the exposure to unexpectedly long life spans and exhaustion of retirees' assets. In general, research in subsequent years has also reported favorable results. Scholz and colleagues, after combining a life-cycle model and optimal decision rules to compare actual and predicted wealth holdings for a representative sample of households from the Health and Retirement Survey (HRS), concluded that fewer that 20 percent of households have inadequate levels of wealth accumulation (Scholz, Seshadri, and Khitatrakun 2006). Hurd and Rohwedder (2008) compared consumption in the early years of retirement with a comprehensive measure of wealth for households in the HRS and argued that the vast majority will be able to sustain their consumption in future years. Some narrowly defined groups, such as singles with less than a high school education, face a need to reduce consumption or risk exhausting their wealth.

A less favorable evaluation is provided by the Center for Retirement Research at Boston College. Its analysis is based on the same SCF wealth data discussed above, but researchers converted from the measure of wealth to an expected level of income in retirement, using a procedure that explicitly incorporates the decline in annuity rates. The projected retirement income for all households in the SCF was then compared to a measure of needs based on the level of pre-retirement consumption.[19] The center constructed the National Retirement Risk Index (NRRI), which classifies a household as being at risk if its retirement income is projected to fall more than 10 percent below its needs (Munnell, Webb, and Golub-Sass 2007). The construction of the index has a number of somewhat arbitrary assumptions, but it has the benefit of providing a consistent time series that reveals how retirement preparedness may have changed over time. It also has the advantage of explicitly incorporating the fall in annuity rates. Hence it provides a more time-consistent measure of retirement income. The index shows a gradual increase in the proportion of households at risk of having inadequate retirement income, from 31 percent in 1983 to 44 percent in 2007 and then to 51 percent in a sharp jump in the midst of the 2008–09 financial crisis (Munnell, Webb,

19. The estimate of required income does fall at retirement because of the exclusion of employment taxes, saving, and the drop in some costs, such as mortgage costs.

and Golub-Sass 2009).[20] The NRRI indicates a substantial impact of the financial crisis on households even though many have few or no significant financial assets. In part, it reflects the loss of homeowners' equity, which limits their ability to make use of a reverse mortgage in retirement.

A recent estimate of the effects of the crisis on the near-retirement population (Gustman, Steinmeier, and Tabatabai 2010) suggests more minimal effects. Based on data from the HRS prior to the crisis, the authors asserted that equities made up only about 15 percent of the group's wealth and that many had already paid off their home mortgage debts. They concluded that the effect of stock market changes on retirement decisions would be small. Hurd and Rohwedder argue for larger costs on the basis of a 2009 Internet survey of HRS participants (Hurd and Rohwedder 2010). Respondents reported larger average declines in consumption than in prior years and major losses for their equity holdings and home values. The fraction of homeowners with a negative equity position in their home quadrupled. They also anticipated a 20 percent reduction in planned future bequests, but that effect was highly concentrated among high-wealth households.

This analysis focuses on the adequacy of wealth for retirement and its impact on consumer spending. Other studies have begun to emphasize a different dimension of saving—its role in providing households with the resources to withstand unanticipated financial shocks, an issue that is often discussed in terms of financial fragility. While large wealth holdings are almost always associated with households in the upper portions of the income distribution, a consideration of financial fragility does demonstrate the relevancy of wealth accumulation even for those at the bottom of the income distribution. Lusardi, Schneider, and Tufano (2010) finds a surprisingly large number of households that live close to the edge and would not be able to come up with even relatively small amounts of money to meet an economic emergency.

Summing Up

The elderly achieved large improvements in their incomes relative to younger households in the 1970s and maintained those gains over the period of reduced saving that began in the mid-1980s. Wealth-income

---

20. A similar type of analysis is undertaken by the Employee Benefit Research Institute (VanDerhei and Copeland 2010)

ratios were stable or rising for all age groups up to the financial crisis of 2008–09, and unusually large capital gains on both equities and home values were sufficient to offset the cumulative effects of reduced saving. The period was marked, however, by an equally dramatic fall in real interest rates and a substantial increase in life expectancies; both factors suggest a greatly reduced flow of annuitized income from a given quantity of wealth. Many of the studies of retirement preparedness emphasized the wealth gains and underplayed the role of the fall in annuity rates, leading them to conclude that older households were relatively well prepared for retirement. Particularly in the aftermath of the financial crisis, the economic well-being of the baby boom generation may be less favorable than suggested in the retirement research.

It is too early to make an informed judgment about the costs of the financial crisis for future retirees. Equity markets have recovered some of their lost value, but home prices have fallen by a third relative to their 2005 peak. The international experiences suggest that the financial crisis will have long-term effects on both the level and rate of growth of incomes, and interest rates will remain at depressed levels for years to come. The impact on public sector finances also leaves the nation much less able to supplement the retirement incomes of the elderly. It is possible that future assessments of retirement preparedness will be less favorable than in the past.

Final Thoughts

The financial crisis has been an enormous shock to the economy of the United States, greatly altering the future outlook. If the performance of other countries is any indicator, the costs will continue in both a permanently lower level of future income and a slower future rate of growth (Abiad and others 2009). Japan, for example, has struggled with recovery from its financial crisis of the early 1990s for the past two decades.

One of the most obvious changes is in the patterns of saving and investment. Expansion of the domestic economy, fueled by a consumption boom, has come to an abrupt end. Martin Feldstein and other researchers have long suggested that the low household saving rate contained the seeds of its own recovery (Feldstein 2006). The negative influence of low saving on household wealth accumulation could not be offset indefinitely by the extraordinary pace of capital gains in the 1990s and early 2000s. Equity and home prices were far above their normal relationships to aggregate income and could be expected to revert to more normal values. The surprise is that it occurred so abruptly. Households will need to devote the remainder of this decade to rebuilding their wealth positions, and the process is already evident in the substantial rise of the household saving rate, to the range of 5 to 6 percent. In the short run, household consumption has been sustained by massive government budget deficits and the transfer of income to households through tax reductions and transfer payments. Thus, the concern with a low rate of private saving has been replaced by worries about unsustainable public sector dissaving. In the aggregate, the United States has had a negative net national saving rate since the onset of the financial crisis, and it now relies on foreign resource inflows to finance all of its capital accumulation and a portion of its consumption.

Much of the fiscal support has been designed to offset the collapse of domestic investment. At the depths of the recent recession, overall GDP had fallen about 6 percent below potential GDP, and about two-thirds of that shortfall was in investment. Residential investment is likely to remain depressed for the remainder of the decade, and business investment will recover only when growth in domestic production eliminates some of the current excess capacity.

Having reached the limits of an economy fueled by excessive consumer spending and a real estate bubble, the United States is now faced with the necessity of restructuring its economy to shift resources out of the domestic sector into net exports. It can no longer afford the large external deficits of the past. Perversely, the collapse of global trade during the crisis actually had a net stabilizing effect: the fall in imports was much larger than the fall in exports and the current account deficit shrank, effectively buffering the fall in domestic production. With recovery, however, the trade deficit has again begun to widen. In the near term, an improvement in the trade balance is consistent with low or negative national saving only as long as investment remains at depressed levels. Like many other countries, the United States would like to engineer an export-led economic recovery, but that will be hard to do given the weakness of its major markets and over two decades of allowing its export capability to wither.

Finally, the optimistic projections of just a few years ago about the economic well-being of future retirees now seem seriously dated. Maybe a few economists would still argue that housing is not wealth and that fluctuations in its price are of little consequence, but that ignores the integrated nature of home values and mortgage financing. Also, even if new retirees do succeed in recovering some of their wealth losses, the continued low level of interest rates suggests that the future flow of income from that wealth will be much less than previously anticipated. The financial crisis has left Americans much less wealthy, both in terms of the market value of their wealth and expectations of future incomes.

References

Abiad, A., and others. 2009. "What's the Damage? Medium-Term Output Dynamics after Banking Crises." International Monetary Fund Working Paper 09/245. Washington: IMF.

Abraham, Katharine. 2010. "Accounting for Investments in Human Capital." *Survey of Current Business* 90, no. 6: 42–53.

Aron, Janine, and others. 2010. "Credit, Housing Collateral, and Consumption: Evidence from the UK, Japan, and the US." CEPR Discussion Paper DP7876. London.

Athukorala, Prema-Chandra, and Kunal Sen. 2004. "The Determinants of Private Saving in India." *World Development* 32, no. 3: 491–503.

Attanasio, Orazio. 1998. "Cohort Analysis of Saving Behavior by U.S. Households." *Journal of Human Resources* 33, no. 3: 575–609.

Auerbach, Alan. 1985. "Saving in the U.S.: Some Conceptual Issues." In *The Level and Composition of Household Saving,* edited by Patric H. Hendershott, pp. 15–38. Cambridge, Mass.: Harper and Row, Ballinger.

Auerbach, Alan, Jinyong Cai, and Laurence Kotlikoff. 1991. "U.S. Demographics and Saving: Predictions of Three Saving Models." Carnegie-Rochester Conference Series on Public Policy (Spring), pp. 135–56.

Auerbach, Alan, and Kevin Hassett. 1999. "Corporate Saving and Shareholder Consumption." In *National Saving and Economic Performance,* edited by D. Bernheim and J. Shoven, pp. 75–98. University of Chicago Press.

Aziz, Jahangir, and Li Cui. 2007. "Explaining China's Low Consumption: The Neglected Role of Household Income." IMF Working Paper 07/181. Washington: IMF.

Bai, Chong-En, and Zhenjie Qian. 2009. "Factor Income Share in China: The Story behind the Statistics." *Economic Research Journal* 3: 27–40.

Baily, Martin Neil, and Robert Z. Lawrence. 2006. "Competitiveness and the Assessment of Trade Performance." In *C. Fred Bergsten and the World Economy,* edited by Michael Mussa. Washington: Peterson Institute for International Economics.

Baker, Malcolm, Stefan Nagel, and Jeffrey Wurgler. 2007. "The Effect of Dividends on Consumption." *BPEA*, no. 1: 231–92.

Barro, Robert. 1974. "Are Government Bonds Net Wealth?" *Journal of Political Economy* 82, no. 6: 1095–117.

Beach, C., R. Boadway, and N. Bruce. 1988. *Taxation and Savings in Canada*. Economic Council of Canada.

Bernanke, Ben S. 2005. "The Global Saving Glut and the U.S. Current Account Deficit." Remarks at the Sanridge Lecture. Richmond, Va.: Virginia Association of Economists (March).

Bernheim, B. Douglas. 1991. *The Vanishing Nest Egg: Reflections on Saving in America*. New York: Twentieth Century Fund.

Bertaut, Carol, Steven Kamin, and Charles Thomas. 2009. "How Long Can the Unsustainable U.S. Current Account Deficit Be Sustained?" *IMF Staff Papers* 56, no. 3: 596–632.

Bérubé, G., and D. Côté. 2000. "Long-Term Determinants of the Personal Saving Rate: Literature Review and Some Empirical Results for Canada." Bank of Canada Working Paper 2000-3. Ottawa: Bank of Canada.

Bhatia, Kul. 1970. "Accrued Capital Gains, Personal Income, and Saving in the United States, 1948–1964." *Review of Income and Wealth* 16, no. 4: 363–78.

Board of Governors of the Federal Reserve. 2010. *Survey of Consumer Finances: 2007* (and prior years) (www.federalreserve.gov/econresdata/scf/scfindex.htm).

———. 2011a. *Flow of Funds Accounts of the United States* (September) (www.federalreserve.gov/releases/z1/current/z1.pdf).

———. 2011b. "Summary Measures of the Foreign Exchange Value of the Dollar: Real Indexes, Broad" (www.federalreserve.gov/releases/h10/summary/default.htm).

Börsch-Supan, Axel, and Annamaria Lusardi. 2003. "Saving: Cross-National Perspective." In *Life-Cycle Savings and Public Policy: A Cross-National Study in Six Countries,* edited by Axel Börsch-Supan. Academic Press.

Boskin, Michael, and Lawrence Lau. 1988. *An Analysis of Postwar U.S. Consumption and Savings Behavior*. Unpublished paper. Stanford University.

Bosworth, Barry, and Rosanna Smart. 2009. "Evaluating Microsurvey Estimates of Wealth and Saving." Working Paper 2009-4. Center for Retirement Research, Boston College.

Bosworth, Barry, Gary Burtless, and John Sabelhaus. 1991. "The Decline in Saving: Some Microeconomic Evidence." *BPEA*, no. 1:183–256.

Bradford, David. 1991. "Market Value and Financial Accounting Measures of National Saving." In *National Saving and Economic Performance,* edited by B. Douglas Bernheim and John B. Shoven, pp. 15-48. University of Chicago Press.

Brown, Jeffrey R., and others. 2001. *The Role of Annuity Markets in Financing Retirement*. MIT Press.

Browning, Martin, and Annamaria Lusardi. 1996. "Household Saving: Micro Theories and Micro Facts." *Journal of Economic Literature* 34, no. 4: 1797–1855.

Buiter, Wilhelm. 2008. "Housing Wealth Is Not Wealth." Working Paper 14204. Cambridge, Mass.: National Bureau of Economic Research.

Burbidge, John, Deborah Fretz, and Michael Veall. 1998. "Canadian and American Saving Rates and the Role of RRSPs." *Canadian Public Policy—Analyse de Politiques* 24, no. 2: 259–63.

Bureau of Economic Analysis. 2011a. *National Income and Product Tables* (www.bea.gov/iTable/index_nipa.cfm).

———. 2011b. "International Investment Position of the United States at Year-End, 1976–2010" (www.bea.gov/international/index.htm#iip).

Bureau of Labor Statistics. 2011. "Consumer Expenditure Survey: Expenditure Tables" (www.bls.gov/cex/csxstnd.htm).

Burtless, Gary, and Eric Toder. 2010. "The Shrinking Tax Preference for Pension Savings: An Analysis of Income Tax Changes, 1985–2007." Working Paper 2010-3. Center for Retirement Research, Boston College.

Carroll, Christopher D. 1997. "Buffer Stock Saving and the Life Cycle/Permanent Income Hypothesis." *Quarterly Journal of Economics* 112 (February): 1–55.

———. 2001. "A Theory of the Consumption Function, with and without Liquidity Constraints." *Journal of Economic Perspectives* 15 (Summer): 23–46.

Carroll, Christopher D., Misuzu Otsuka, and Jiri Slacalek. 2011. "How Large Are Housing and Financial Wealth Effects? A New Approach." *Journal of Money, Credit, and Banking* 43, no. 1: 55–79.

Carroll, Christopher D., and Andrew A. Samwick. 1997. "The Nature of Precautionary Wealth." *Journal of Monetary Economics* 40 (September): 41–71.

Carroll, Christopher, and Lawrence Summers. 1987. "Why Have Private Savings Rates in the United States and Canada Diverged?" *Journal of Monetary Economics* 20, no. 2: 249–79.

Case, Karl E., John M. Quigley, and Robert J. Shiller. 2005. "Comparing Wealth Effects: The Stock Market versus the Housing Market." *Advances in Macroeconomics* 5, no. 1: 1–34.

Central Statistical Office. 2010. *New Series of National Account Statistics (Base Year 2004–05)*. Government of India, Ministry of Statistics and Program Implementation.

Chamon, Marcos, and Eswar Prasad. 2008. "Why Are Saving Rates of Urban Households in China Rising?" Working Paper 14546. Cambridge, Mass.: National Bureau of Economic Research.

Cline, William R. 2005. *The United States as a Debtor Nation*. Washington: Institute for International Economics.

Congressional Budget Office. 2003. *Baby Boomers Retirement Prospects: An Overview*. Congress of the United States (November).

————. 2008. *The Outlook for Housing Starts: 2009 to 2012.* Congress of the United States (November).

————. 2011. *The Budget and Economic Outlook: Fiscal Years 2011 to 2021* (January).

Corrado, Carol, Charles Hulten, and Daniel Sichel. 2005. "Measuring Capital and Technology: An Expanded Framework." In *Measuring Capital in the New Economy,* edited by C. Corrado, J. Haltwinger, and D. Sichel, pp. 11–41. Cambridge, Mass.: National Bureau of Economic Research.

Cuaresma, Jesús Crespo, and Gerhard Reitschuler. 2007. "Is the Ricardian Equivalence Proposition an 'Aerie Fairy' Theory for Europe?" *Economica* 74, no. 296: 682–94.

Deaton, Angus S. 1991. "Saving and Liquidity Constraints." *Econometrica* 59 (September): 1121–42.

————. 1992. *Understanding Consumption.* Oxford University Press.

Denison, Edward F. 1958. "A Note on Private Saving." *Review of Economics and Statistics* 40: 761–67.

Dynan, Karen E. 2009. "Changing Household Financial Opportunities and Economic Security." *Journal of Economic Perspectives* 23, no. 4: 49–68.

Economic and Social Research Institute. 2011. *National Accounts for 2009.* Tokyo: Cabinet Office of Japan.

Edwards, Sebastian. 2005. "Is the U.S. Current Account Deficit Sustainable? If Not, How Costly Is Adjustment Likely to Be?" *BPEA,* no. 1: 211–28.

Eisner, Robert. 1989. *The Total Income System of Accounts.* University of Chicago Press.

————. 1991. "The Real Rate of National Saving." *Review of Income and Wealth,* Series 37, no. 1 (March): 15–32.

Engelhardt, Gary. 1996a. "House Prices and Home Owner Saving Behavior." *Regional Science and Urban Economics* 26: 313–36.

————. 1996b. "Tax Subsidies and Household Saving: Evidence from Canada." *Quarterly Journal of Economics* 111, no. 4: 1237–68.

Engelhardt, Gary, and Anil Kumar. 2007. "Pensions and Household Wealth Accumulation." Working Paper. Maxwell School, Syracuse University.

Federal Reserve Bank of Philadelphia. 2011. "Third Quarter 2011 Survey of Professional Forecasters." Philadelphia (August).

Feldstein, Martin. 1974. "Social Security, Induced Retirement, and Aggregate Capital Accumulation." *Journal of Political Economy* 82, no. 5: 905–26.

————. 1985. "American Economic Policy and the World Economy." *Foreign Affairs* 63, no. 5: 995–1008.

————. 2006. "The Return of Saving." *Foreign Affairs* 85, no. 3: 87–93.

Feldstein, Martin, and Charles Horioka. 1980. "Domestic Saving and International Capital Flows." *Economic Journal* 90, no. 358 (June): 314–29.

Fisher, T. Lynn. 2007. "Estimates of Unreported Asset Income in the Survey of Consumer Finances and the Relative Importance of Social Security Benefits to the Elderly." *Social Security Bulletin* 67, no. 2: 47–53.

Frankel, Jeffrey. 1992. "Measuring Capital Mobility: A Review." *American Economic Association Papers and Proceedings* 82, no. 2, pp. 197–202.

Gale, William G. 2005. "The Impact of Pensions and 401(k) Plans on Households' Saving and Wealth." In *The Evolving Pension System: Trends, Effects, and Proposals for Reform,* edited by William G. Gale, John B. Shoven, and Mark J. Warshawsky, pp. 103–21. Brookings.

Gale, William, and Karen Pence. 2006. "Are Successive Generations Getting Wealthier, and If So, Why? Evidence from the 1990s." *BPEA,* no.1: 155–234.

Gale, William G., and John Sabelhaus. 1999. "Perspectives on the Household Saving Rate." *BPEA,* no. 1: 181–223.

Garner, Thesia, Robert McClelland, and William Passero. 2009. "Strengths and Weaknesses of the Consumer Expenditure Survey from a BLS Perspective." Paper presented at the National Bureau of Economic Research, Summer Institute Conference on Research on Income and Wealth (June).

Gokhale, Jagadeesh, Laurence Kotlikoff, and John Sabelhaus.1996. "Understanding the Postwar Decline in U.S. Saving: A Cohort Analysis." *BPEA,* no. 1: 315–407.

Greenspan, Alan, and James Kennedy. 2008. "Sources and Uses of Equity Extracted from Homes." *Oxford Review of Economic Policy* 24, no 1: 120–44.

Gustman, Alan L., Thomas L. Steinmeier, and Nahid Tabatabai. 2010. "What the Stock Market Decline Means for the Financial Security and Retirement Choices of the Near-Retirement Population." *Journal of Economic Perspectives* 24, no. 1: 161–82.

Hall, Robert E. 2000. "E-Capital: The Link between the Stock Market and the Labor Market in the 1990s." *BPEA,* no. 2: 73–118.

Hayashi, Fumio. 1986. "Why Is Japan's Saving Rate So Apparently High?" In *NBER Macroeconomics Annual,* vol. 1, edited by Stanley Fischer, pp. 147–210. Cambridge, Mass.: National Bureau of Economic Research.

———. 1997. *Understanding Saving: Evidence from the United States and Japan.* MIT Press.

Hendershott, Patric H., and Joe Peek. 1989. "Aggregate U.S. Private Saving: Conceptual Measures." In *The Measurement of Saving, Investment, and Wealth.* Studies in Income and Wealth, vol. 52, edited by Robert E. Lipsey and Helen Stone Tice, pp. 185–223. University of Chicago Press.

Horioka, Charles Yuji. 1989. "Why Is Japan's Private Saving Rate So High?" In *Developments in Japanese Economics,* edited by Ryuzo Sato and Takashi Negishi, pp. 145–78. Tokyo: Academic Press/Harcourt Brace Jovanovich.

———. 1991. "The Determinants of Japan's Saving Rate: The Impact of the Age Structure of the Population and Other Factors." *Economic Studies Quarterly* [now *Japanese Economic Review*] 42, no. 3: 237–53.

———. 1996. "Capital Gains in Japan: Their Magnitude and Impact on Consumption." *Economic Journal* 106, no. 436 (May): 560–77.

———. 1997. "A Co-integration Analysis of the Impact of the Age Structure of the Population on the Household Saving Rate in Japan." *Review of Economics and Statistics* 79, no. 3: 511–16.

———. 2010. "The (Dis)saving Behavior of the Aged in Japan." *Japan and the World Economy* 22, no. 3: 151–58.

Hüfner, Felix, and Isabell Koske. 2010. "Explaining Household Saving Rates in G7 Countries: Implications for Germany." OECD Economics Department Working Paper 754. Paris: OECD.

Hurd, Michael D., and Susann Rohwedder. 2008. "The Adequacy of Economic Resources in Retirement." MRRC Working Paper 2008-184. Ann Arbor: Michigan Retirement Research Center.

———. 2010. "The Effects of the Economic Crisis on the Older Population." MRRC Working Paper 2010-231. Ann Arbor: Michigan Retirement Research Center.

International Monetary Fund. 1995. *World Economic Outlook.* Washington (May).

———. 2007. "The Globalization of Labor." *World Economic Outlook.* Washington (April).

———. 2009. *World Economic Outlook.* Washington (October).

———. 2011a. *World Economic Outlook.* Washington (April).

———. 2011b. *International Financial Statistics.* Washington.

Jorgenson, Dale, and Barbara Fraumeni. 1989. "The Accumulation of Human and Nonhuman Capital, 1948–84." In *The Measurement of Saving, Investment, and Wealth,* Studies in Income and Wealth, vol. 52, edited by Robert E. Lipsey and Helen Stone Tice. University of Chicago Press.

Jorgenson, D. W., J. S. Landefeld, W. D. Nordhaus. 2006. "A New Architecture for the U.S. National Accounts." University of Chicago Press.

JP Morgan. 2011. "Real Effective Exchange Rate Index." Data on file with author.

Jump, Gregory V. 1980. "Interest Rates, Inflation Expectations, and Spurious Elements in Measured Real Income and Saving." *American Economic Review* 70: 990–1004.

Jump, G. V., and T. A. Wilson. 1986. "Savings in Canada: Retrospective and Prospective." In *Economic Growth: Prospects and Determinants,* edited by John Sargent. University of Toronto Press.

Juster, F. Thomas, and others. 2006. "The Decline in Household Saving and the Wealth Effect." *Review of Economics and Statistics* 88, no.1: 20–27.

Kendrick, John. 1961. *Productivity Trends in the United States.* New York: National Bureau of Economic Research.

————. 1976. *The Formation and Stocks of Total Capital*. New York: National Bureau of Economic Research.

Koga, Maiko. 2006. "The Decline of Japan's Saving Rate and Demographic Effects." *Japanese Economic Review* 57, no. 2: 312–21.

Kuijs, Louis. 2006. "How Will China's Saving-Investment Balance Evolve?" World Bank Policy Research Working Paper 3958. Washington: World Bank (July).

Lipsey, Robert E., and Irving B. Kravis. 1987. *Saving and Economic Growth: Is the United States Really Falling Behind?* New York: Conference Board.

Lusardi, Annamaria, Daniel Schneider, and Peter Tufano. 2011. "Financially Fragile Households: Evidence and Implications." *BPEA*, no. 1: 83–150.

Ma, Guonan, and Wang Yi. 2010. "China's High Saving Rate: Myth and Reality." Working Paper 312. Basel, Switzerland: Bank for International Settlements (June).

McKinsey Global Institute. 1994. *The Global Capital Market: Supply, Demand, Pricing, and Allocation*. Washington.

Millwood, Kevin. 2002. "Tax-Preferred Savings Accounts and Marginal Tax Rates: Evidence on RRSP Participation." *Canadian Journal of Economics* 35, no. 3: 436–56.

Mishra, Deepak. 2006. "Can India Attain the East Asian Growth with a South Asian Saving Rate?" Paper presented at ICRIER–World Bank Conference, New Delhi, May.

Modigliani, F., and R. Brumberg. 1954. "Utility Analysis and the Consumption Function: An Interpretation of Cross-Section Data." In *Post-Keynesian Economics*, edited by K. Kurihara, pp. 388–436. Rutgers University Press.

Muellbauer, John. 2007. "Housing, Credit and Consumer Expenditure." CEPR Discussion Paper 6782.

Munnell, Alicia H., Anthony Webb, and Francesca Golub-Sass. 2007. "Is There Really a Retirement Savings Crisis? An NRRI Analysis." Issues in Brief 2007-7-11. Boston College, Center for Retirement Research (August).

————. 2009. "The National Retirement Risk Index: After the Crash." Issues in Brief 9-22. Boston College, Center for Retirement Research.

National Bureau of Statistics of China. 2011. *China Statistical Yearbook: 2011*. Beijing.

National Science Foundation. 2010. *National Patterns of R&D Resources: 2008 Data Update* (www.nsf.gov/statistics/nsf10314/).

Obstfeld, Maurice, and Kenneth Rogoff. 1996. *Foundations of International Macroeconomics*. MIT Press.

————. 2004. "The Unsustainable U.S. Current Account Position Revisited." Working Paper 10869. Cambridge, Mass.: National Bureau of Economic Research.

Okubo, Sumiye, and others. 2006. "BEA's 2006 Research and Development Satellite Account." *Survey of Current Business* 86, no. 12: 14–44.

Organization for Economic Cooperation and Development. 1996. *Future Global Capital Shortages: Real Threat or Pure Fiction?* Paris.

———. 2007. "Corporate Saving and Investment: Recent Trends and Prospects." *OECD Economic Outlook* 82: 191–212 (December).

———. 2011. OECD.Stat (database). (www.oecd-ilibrary.org/economics/data/oecd-stat_data-00285-en).

Ortalo-Magne, Francois, and Sven Rady. 2002. "Tenure Choice and the Riskiness of Non-Housing Consumption." *Journal of Housing Economics* 11, no. 3: 266–79.

Panel Study of Income Dynamics. 2011. Public use dataset. University of Michigan, Institute for Social Research.

Park, Donghyun, and Kwanho Shin. 2009. "Saving, Investment, and Current Account Surplus in Developing Asia." ADB Economics Working Paper Series 158. Manila: Asian Development Bank (April).

Parker, Jonathan A. 2000. "Spendthrift in America? On Two Decades of a Decline in the U.S. Saving Rate." In *NBER Macroeconomics Annual: 1999*, edited by Ben S. Bernanke and Julio J. Rotemberg. MIT Press.

Peach, Richard, and Charles Steindel. 2000. "A Nation of Spendthrifts? An Analysis of Trends in Personal and Gross Saving." *Current Issues in Economics and Finance* [Federal Reserve Bank of New York] 6, no. 2: 1–6.

Perotti, Roberto. 1999. "Fiscal Policy in Good Times and Bad." *Quarterly Journal of Economics* 114, no. 4: 1399–1436.

Perozek, Maria, and Marshall Reinsdorf. 2002. "Alternative Measures of Personal Saving." *Survey of Current Business* 82 (April): 13–24.

Pichette, L., and D. Tremblay. 2003. "Are Wealth Effects Important for Canada?" Bank of Canada Working Paper 2003-30. Ottawa: Bank of Canada.

Poterba, James M. 1987. "Tax Policy and Corporate Saving." *BPEA*, no. 2: 455–515.

———. 2000. "Stock Market Wealth and Consumption." *Journal of Economic Perspectives* 14, no. 2: 99–118.

Projector, Dorothy. 1968. *Survey of Changes in Family Finances*. Federal Reserve Technical Papers. Washington: Board of Governors of the Federal Reserve System.

Ricciuti, Ricardo. 2003. "Assessing Ricardian Equivalence." *Journal of Economic Surveys* 17, no. 1: 55–78.

Röhn, Oliver. 2010. "New Evidence on the Private Saving Offset and Ricardian Equivalence." OECD Economics Department Working Papers 762.

Romer, Christina. 1990. "The Great Crash and the Onset of the Great Depression." *Quarterly Journal of Economics* 105, no. 3: 597–624.

Ruggles, Richard, and Nancy D. Ruggles. 1982. "Integrated Economic Accounts for the United States, 1947–80." *Survey of Current Business* 62 (5): 1–53.

Saez, Emmanuel, and Michael R. Veall. 2005. "The Evolution of High Incomes in Northern America: Lessons from Canadian Evidence." *American Economic Review* 95, no. 3: 831–49.

Scholz, John Karl, Ananth Seshadri, and Surachai Khitatrakun. 2006. "Are Americans Saving 'Optimally' for Retirement?" *Journal of Political Economy* 114 (August): 607–43.

Sinai, Todd, and Nicholas S. Souleles. 2005. "Owner-Occupied Housing as a Hedge against Rent Risk." Working Paper 9462. Cambridge, Mass.: National Bureau of Economic Research.

Slacalek, Jiri. 2009. "What Drives Personal Consumption? The Role of Housing and Financial Wealth." *B.E. Journal of Macroeconomics* 9, no. 1 (www. bepress.com/bejm/vol9/iss1/art37).

Slesnick, Daniel. 1992. "Aggregate Consumption and Saving in the Postwar United States." *Review of Economics and Statistics* 74, no.4: 585–97.

Spence, A. Michael. 1973."Job Market Signaling." *Quarterly Journal of Economics* 87, no. 3: 355–74.

Statistics Canada. 2011a. *National Balance Sheet Accounts.* Ottawa

———. 2011b. *National Income and Expenditure Accounts.* Ottawa

———. 2011c. *Survey of Household Spending.* Microdata set. Ottawa.

Tobin, James. 1967. "Life Cycle Saving and Balanced Growth." In *Ten Economic Studies in the Tradition of Irving Fisher,* pp. 231–56. New York: John Wiley.

United Nations. 2009. *World Population Prospects: 2008 Revision.* New York.

———. 2011. *World Population Prospects: 2010 Revision* (http://esa.un.org/ unpd/wpp/index.htm).

U.S. Social Security Administration. 2011. *Income of the Population 55 and Older: 1990 and 2008.* Office of Retirement and Disability Policy (www.ssa. gov/policy/docs/statcomps/income_pop55/).

VanDerhei, Jack, and Craig Copeland. 2010. "The EBRI Retirement Readiness Rating:™ Retirement Income Preparation and Future Prospects." *EBRI Issue Brief* 344. Employee Benefit Research Institute (July).

Verma, Satyendra, and Jules Lichtenstein. 2006. "Pension Lump-Sum Distributions: Do Booomers Take Them or Save Them?" Washington: AARP Public Policy Institute (http://assets.aarp.org/rgcenter/econ/dd144_pension.pdf).

Volcker, Paul A. 1984. "Facing Up to the Twin Deficits." *Challenge* (March-April): 4–9.

World Bank. 2011. *World Development Indicators.* Washington.

Zeldes, Stephen. 1989. "Consumption and Liquidity Constraints: An Empirical Investigation." *Journal of Political Economy* 97 (April): 305–46.

Index

BROOKINGS The Brookings Institution is a private nonprofit organization devoted to research, education, and publication on important issues of domestic and foreign policy. Its principal purpose is to bring the highest quality independent research and analysis to bear on current and emerging policy problems. The Institution was founded on December 8, 1927, to merge the activities of the Institute for Government Research, founded in 1916, the Institute of Economics, founded in 1922, and the Robert Brookings Graduate School of Economics and Government, founded in 1924. Interpretations or conclusions in Brookings publications should be understood to be solely those of the authors.
